Monte di Pietà

edited by
Giancarlo Alisio

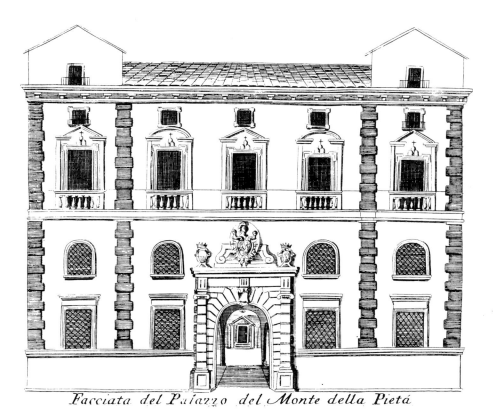

Facciata del Palazzo del Monte della Pietà

EDIZIONE
BANCO di NAPOLI

THE PRESENT VOLUME HAS BEEN EDITED BY EDIZIONI SCIENTIFICHE ITALIANE

TRANSLATION BY BRUNA DI SABATO

PHOTOGRAPHS BY MASSIMO VELO

PHOTOGRAPHS BY MONICA MARTELLI-CASTALDI (pp. 118 - 122 - 123 - 124 - 126 - 127 - 128 - 132)

Introduction

This volume testifies to the will of our institution to become a bank with new geographical and operative borders without putting aside the old traditions that gave the Banco di Napoli *the opportunity to grow uninterruptedly since 1539. Our institution has tried to follow the profound changes occurring in the world financial and banking scene not only participating actively in the internationalization process, but also sustaining and evaluating culture in its several forms of expression.*

The strategy of geographical and operative development has been realized both through the expansion of our foreign network and through the growing importance achieved by currency investments on the total budget (44.6% at the close of 1986).

A branch in Hong Kong and an agency in Los Angeles have been added to the four already existing foreign branches - New York, Buenos Aires, Frankfurt and London. These are operative bases that in the short/medium terms will allow the Banco di Napoli *to take an active part in the process of intensive development that is being realized on the Pacific Ocean markets.*

Undoubtedly, the strongest point in the Banco di Napoli's *foreign activity is represented by the New York branch. At the beginning of this century ours was among the first European banks to settle in the United States in order to support all those resources that at the time were flowing towards the largest North-American market from the South of Italy.*

Once accomplished the task it was created for, the branch in New York continued to work as an important agency of the bank till the first half of the seventies not yet well connected with the internal American productive market. Today, after only ten years from the onset of its operative activity, the branch is not only a force in inter-bank relations but of the loan market to productive concerns as well it is to be added that according to the most recent official statistics, the branch of New York is the first Italian bank with respect to "commercial and industrial loans", it ranks second among the European banks and eighth among the foreign ones.

On the occasion of the decennial of the New York branch, the Banco di Napoli *publishes this volume in order to pay homage to its more qualified colleagues in the United States who in the following pages will find a detailed description of the restoration of the noble building of the* Monte di Pietà. *This building is not only an historical landmark for our bank but was a haven for those forefathers who could solve their difficulties there in an epoch which offered little other solution. The* Monte di Pietà *was, in fact, the seat of one of the first public banks in Naples, eventually fusing with other banks to give rise to the present day* Banco di Napoli. *It was created in 1539 by two Neapolitan noblemen - its primary philanthropic aim to halt the phenomenon of usury which was widespread at that time.*

For the Banco di Napoli *today, the restoration of the building and the chapel of the* Monte di Pietà *means rediscovering its roots, a sort of "return to the ancestral* home" in pursuit of stimuli for ever more incisive development. In fact, the turning-point in the managerial imprint of 1983, aimed at a more dynamic activity of the bank on national and international markets, has cancelled neither the consciousness of being guardian of historical values having their roots in the South of Italy nor the awareness that the development of this area requires enormous financial resources, a problem that the bank has frequently tried to solve in more recent years.

We have not to forget that Naples could be named among the cultural capitals of Europe. The restoration of the Monte di Pietà can be seen as part of a large plan of socio-cultural impulse to Southern Italy whose main supporter is the Banco di Napoli.

Such an engagement aims both at giving financial assistance to public institutions having the task of caring for and restorating famous monuments, and at promoting new initiatives. One of these is the artistic patrimony that the Banco di Napoli has gathered during some four centuries. An international body of experts has advised the bank to purchase, among other things, a rich and until now unknown series of oils on canvas by Anton Smink Pitloo which is rare indeed. Moreover, the Banco di Napoli bought a valuable still-life by G.B. Ruoppolo and an important work by H. Van Somer. The bank is also interested in the so-called «arti minori» which stem from popular tradition: for instance an important collection of crib figures which has been successively enlarged. The main aim is to diffuse the knowledge of such art in foreign countries as well thanks to an exhibition and to a publication. This will be appreciated not only by Southern Italians who consider the crib one of their most valuable cultural expressions but also by everyone who is interested in the study of both individual and collective primitive artistic expressions.

Moreover, a series of fixed meetings has been taking place over the last four years aimed at evaluating the ties existing between the bank and society through a well-advised dialogue with all the branches of culture from economics to science to literary research.

Whatever the direction taken by these meetings, the main point has been the exploration of the most lively levels of our society, pointing out the most important problems and, in so doing, helping to contribute to their solution from a managerial point of view. In the light of the success of the meeting on music and historical gardens, a series of musical exhibitions has been organised with great success in the historical gardens of Naples. The meetings about theatre and cinema have given the opportunity to encourage debate about these artistical expressions and, at the same time, to encourage, thanks to the financial assistance of the Banco di Napoli, the re-opening of «Mercadante», an old Neapolitan theatre that had been closed to the public for several years.

In a few words such interventions by the Banco di Napoli aim at emphasising the cultural identity of Naples, considered a genuine and essential point of reference for the city and for the whole of Southern Italy. This engagement equally concerns art, economy, scientific and banking research, conscious as we have always been of the latest achievements of Naples - a city which is a unique moment in universal culture.

Ferdinando Ventriglia
General Manager
of the Banco di Napoli

Luigi Coccioli
President
of the Banco di Napoli

Preface

It is worth noting the activity of the Banco di Napoli *in protecting certain real estate of great historical value. The* Monte di Pietà *is one of these — the old and prestigious seat of one the four credit institutions which gave birth to the* Banco di Napoli.

The building is in the beautiful but badly depreciated historical centre of Naples, rich in precious churches, conventual insulae, noble buildings ruined by now owing to complete lack of any intervention of maintenance and restoration. The Monte di Pietà *rises precisely along the inferior decuman of the ancient Greek city just a few meters from S. Gregorio Armenio street and from the actual S. Gaetano Square, once seat of the «agora» and consequently of the Roman forum. In fact, notwithstanding the presence of several monuments of the ancient centre of the town the most interesting element is the still-existing original urban framework - an «ippodameo» structure with tree decumans running from East to West — along stands the* Monte di Pietà *— and several «cardi» that in, crossing them, define rectangular blocks of the same size.*

Thanks to continuity of the settling of inhabitants and the employment of the already existing buildings as bases for the new activities, the ancient urban distribution not only was not destroyed but it still survives in the old scheme of the streets.

Since 1972 when, in view of specific projects the historical centre — unique monument in the history of human civilization — was separated from the town-planning public institutions have been discussing the possible future of this part of Naples. During these years, spent waiting for something to happen unlawfulness has prevailed, with no objections made to new building interventions. Therefore, every day new buildings rise up and ancient portals and thresholds in vesuvian stone, are replaced with new ones, while flamboyant shops occupy the façades of the building with showy windows contrasting with the ancient openings. All this is conceived in contrast with municipal regulations which should and must obviate them. In this context, the activity of the Banco di Napoli *is even more valuable in that it has shown a way that can be followed by other institutions — for the safeguarding of many of these buildings.*

The Monte di Pietà *was built at the end of the XVI century on the area of the old* Carafa *building. Its construction was part of the important building restoration which took place during the second half of the XVI and the entire XVII century. There were two factors which led to these transformations, on one side the policy of the Spanish viceroys that prevented an organic growth of the city for about a century and a half, with restrictive laws which caused profound and widespread negative effects. On the other side there was the Counter-Reformation, with the arrival of the new religious orders in Naples. These latter with their tendency "a fare insula" — i.e. to be separated from the exterior world — provoked a prevalence of religious buildings over the civil ones which in some areas of the town almost disappeared.*

The Monte di Pietà *required different solutions in comparison to the other public* buildings, owing to its particular activity (i.e. to overcome usury by encouraging loans on pledge with no interest). The important plan was entrusted to Giovan Battista Cavagna who also directed the works for the construction. On the façade, characterised by an accentuated chiaroscuro effect, embossment work has been adopted on the pilasters that the delimit it, on the external openings and on the large portal, while owing to the small space in front of the building — the biggest openings are on the second floor in order to afford more light.

The most striking aspect of the building is the entrance, where the high medium archway frames the façade of the chapel in the background of the court-yard. While the interior of the building, notwithstanding the numerous remains of the frescoes, has been changed throughout the centuries, the chapel with its appeerence of late mannerism has remained untouched. Therefore, today it is a typical example of religious building in the XVII century where painted ceilings, rich decorations and furnishings constitute a delicate and homogeneous whole. Both the façade and the interior decoration were conceived by the "committente" (the clients) who, in 1602, suggested to Belisario Corenzio the sacred scenes to be painted on the vault i.e. the theme of the passion of Christ, one of the favourite episodes of the Counter-Reformation. This gave the painter the possibility expressing his art at its best, with results that rarely again will be reached by the artist.

The main part of the frescoes in gold stucco frames was completed in 1603 and in the same years the three altar-pieces by Scipione Borghese and Fabrizio Santafede were finished as well.

Later, during the XVIII century, some maintenance work was done in the Sacristy and in the "Sala delle Cantoniere".

The ravages of time, wars and frequent earthquakes seriously damaged the frescoes, while the presence of a wall above the vault of the chapel determined static problems. During these years with an expensive and ingenious system of "anchoring" carried out by the technical office of the Banco di Napoli the attic areas above the chapel have been suspended, by stay-rods connected to a trellis placed on the ceiling of the building in order to eliminate the wall and give the vault its original elasticity. Moreover, the frescoes and marble work have been restored, giving back to the chapel its original splendour. These operations of restoration, the deep analysis of the frescoes and sacred furnishings, the significant of the building to Neapolitan architectonic culture between 1500 and 1600, assisted by a rich series of documents found in the Archivio Storico del Banco di Napoli, are what we have tried to present in this volume, hoping that this intervention will not be an isolated episode but that it will be the starting point for a true and meaningful restoration of the historical centre of Naples.

Giancarlo Alisio

Greetings

The austere and stately building of the Monte di Pietà *is admirable indeed, but much more admirable is the governors' wish to create with its chapel « Un gioiello per offrirlo — inno di riconoscenza a Dio, che aveva concesso alla Pia Opera una ascesa tanto prodigiosa». They have succeeded in combining the cold luminosity of marbles with the warmth of charity and the perfume of Christian piety.*
Art has always divined that matter can overcome itself, though it has always employed the matter to express the superiority of the spirit.
In the name of the whole archdiocese of Naples I wish to express my joy to the Banco di Napoli *for the restoration and re-opening of this «tenda di Dio» among the houses of men.*
If it is true that the historical centre reveals the convulsive dynamism of a city, it is also right that a place like this should exist as well — almost an oasis — where the soul finds its space and reflects in silence, prays and learns to love the brothers it meets on its way.

Don Ezio Calabrese
Rector of the Church

G.B. Cavagna and the Architecture of the Building
by Silvana Savarese

From the second half of the XVI century onwards, the protagonists of urban renewal were religious orders; the presence of several architects, especially among the Jesuits and Theatine orders is, obviously determinant to this process.

Ideological consequences of the Counter-reformation, resulted between about 1570 and the first half of XVII century, in a complete turning point in local architectonic production. Not only did this influence the transformation of the town but also it accentuated the already appreciable dichotomy existing between civil and religious buildings, obviously in favour of the latter ones. As soon as the new orders arrived in town, the conventual workshops multiplied in order to restrain the Lutheran and Calvinist tendencies that began to spread in Naples as well during the fourth decade of the century. These tendencies were encouraged by the crisis in the ecclesiastical world that inevitably, influenced every aspect of civilian life[1]. Moreover, the acquisition by religious orders of real estates nearby their sees became characteristic of conventual bodies. In this way, availing themselves of a «diritto mostruoso»[2] and demolishing several civilian buildings[3], they pursued their tendency to «fare isola».

In spite of the new rules that made religious workshops destroy or radically transform the look of the town even more than earthquakes and restorations — so that nowadays we have only a few examples of Byzantine and Romanesque architecture[4] — it is important to note the role architects of the Counter-reformation played in overcoming traditional canons in the absence of a good local culture. Although the religious architects, worked in perfect adherence to tridentine rules in the transformation of old convents and in the building of new ones, they significantly reflect the lexical crisis which took place — for what concerns Neapolitan architecture — after the Council and that will be solved, more or less in the middle of XVII century, thanks to Cosimo Fanzago.

Even if these may often be considered mere peculiarities concerning forms of expression, they contribute to the recover and definition of a tendency in the Neapolitan style, different from that of Norman production of the first decades of XVI century, by that time vanished.

Moreover, these formal characteristics testify to the crisis caused by the attempt to overcome the classical tradition by means of a taste which was far from both the serene equilibrium of Renaissance and the expressive redundancy of baroque. It was a taste only partly resembling those peculiarities of the mannerism typical of Rome and the North and Central Italy, which, for social and cultural reasons spread in the Parthenopean town only later[5].

In this regard, the Roman and Tuscan experience that G.B. Cavagna, D. Fontana, G.A. Dosio and in some measure Vincenzo Casali and Dionisio Nencioni, called «di Bartolomeo», imported between XVI and XVII centuries are much more significant and though indirectly, allowed Naples to take part in the mannerist debate.

G.B. Cavagna is present in Naples both as an architect and as a painter in two different periods of time starting from 1574 when he began the works for the church of *S. Gregorio Armeno*. According to some recent archive findings he presumably produced more than we know today, both in the capital and in the provinces.

Biographical notes about Cavagna are scarce indeed, we neither know when he was born[6] nor his birth-place and though the sources always name him as Roman, his family came from Northern Italy[7].

Besides having worked as an architect, he must have worked a lot as a painter too though only a few of this paintings have survived[8], as stated by G.B. D'Addosio, G. Bresciano and G. Sobotka[9], together with some archive findings about which we will speak later on.

The Church of *S. Gregorio Armeno*, Cavagna's first work in Naples, though not proved by documents, is annexed to the homonymous convent, generally ascribed to Vincenzo Della Monica[10]. Recent studies have established Della Monica to be merely the executor of a plan by G.F. Di Palma[11], acknowledged as the author of the plan for the convent of *S. Marcellino* too[12].

In the single nave of *S. Gregorio Armeno* pilasters with pairs of pilaster-strips alternate with the rather low entrances to the chapels, supporting an uninterrupted trabeation: this structure shows a clear analogy with the church of *Gesù* in Rome. The strict adherence of the structure to Counter-reformation modules almost disappears under the rich decoration of the XVI and XVII centuries; gold stuccos and frescoes that nowadays only leave us a vague idea of the original distribution so that the internal space is one of the more remarkable expressions of the local baroque.

On the contrary, the exterior of the church still shows the original plan of the XVI century; the front, perhaps previously surmounted by a triangular tympanum over the second order, presents three «piperno» arches on a pronaos, where two pairs of pilasters rise up in correspondence with the external ones, supporting a vaulted roof, similar in structure to the one that Cavagna will carry out, though with a different approach, in the *Monte di Pietà* entrance-hall.

After a stay in Rome among the members of the *Accademia di San Luca*[13], Cavagna came back to Naples and, between 1589 and 1591, results to be engaged in the XVI century rebuilding of the church of *S. Paolo Maggiore*, built in 798[14] on the ruins of the Dioscuri Temple.

Possibly the medieval basilica was abandoned for a long time, so that when the Theatines obtained it, in 1538, by intercession of the viceroy Pedro de Toledo, they found it almost destroyed[15].

The work to repair and transform it inside, began in 1581[16], according to a plan, almost unanimously ascribed to Francesco Grimaldi[17] although documentary sources do not confirm this theory.

As we can infer from information found in the *Libro delle Spese* for the construction of the church, the years '83-84 were marked by intense activity. In april 1583 a payment is entered «per il modello della chiesa e parte della sua fattura»[18] and, on the same date some fragmentary information lead us to think that the works went on quite speedily in this period[19]. Also in April the bell-tower and the old choir were dismantled[20] and the next June payments were made «a m° Gio. Lorenzo d'Albano à conto del choro nuovo»[21] and on March, 2nd 1584, «A m° Ant° marmoraro per poner i gradi del Choro e Altare Maggiore e l'Agnello»[22].

Façade of the Building, detail. The narrowness of the street prevents an overall view

In the following years we have no traces of the development of the works and they were resumed only in 1589 as results from «Introiti di Denari che entrano in mano di Don Pietro per la fabbrica del corpo della nostra chiesa di San Paolo. Cominciata sotto la prepositura di R. Pre Don Agostino à 27 luglio 1589» and from payments «a mastri fabricatori et manipoli che han lavorato nella fabbrica della Chiesa nelli fondamenti dalli 27 di luglio per tutti li 12 di agosto...»[23], although the difference between the new part — the apse and the transept — and the old one — the three aisles — separated by the granitic columns of the pagan temple[24] — must have been strong indeed.

Quattrone[25] — like Ceva Grimaldi before him[26] — maintains that P.D. Pietro Caracciolo had been entrusted with the realization of the plan by F. Grimaldi. This could be plausible if we consider that on the 27th of August 1585 F. Grimaldi went to Rome where he stayed for about thirteen years. He could then have settled in that town, going away, from time to time to work elsewhere. So it could be maintained that as Grimaldi was at the building yard only now and then, Caracciolo had replaced him for what concerned the normal direction of the work.

Nevertheless, according to the documents concerning the new phase of the construction G.B. Cavagna results be engaged in the work from the beginning and in the *Libro delle spese* for the construction, already on the 29th July 1589 it is recorded «Pagati in contanti a m. Gio. Bapta Cavagna Architetto in parte dei disegni che ha tirati per la fabrica della Chiesa d. 5.0.0.» and then, in September «Pagati in contanti a m. Gio. Bapta Architetto per il disegno della facciata della Chiesa d. 5.0.0.»[27]. Were these ex novo drawings, or variations of a previous plan?

Monthly payments are entered till the 6th July 1590 when «...ms. Gio. Batta d.ti tre per l'indoratura della pietra negra della chiesa»[28] are paid.

By that time, the XVI. century front had evidently been finished and further confirmation comes from the *Giornali* by Bulifon «...si fece in questo medesimo anno la facciata della chiesa di San Paolo dei Padri Teatini»[29].

It is difficult to reconstruct the appearance of the front, though it is possible to make some hypotheses, starting from the achievements of the single masters working on the construction[30].

The XVI century front — of which we have no pictures — probably anticipated, details, that can be found later in the front of the *Monte di Pietà*, nearly a decade older. For the latter Cavagna referred to the plan by Giovanni Donadio for the front of *S. Maria della Stella*, even if there are chromatic variations with a tinge of baroque. As reference to our hypotesis if we assume the aspect of the successive work by Cavagna, the few elements that can be found in the documents and the proportions of the inside (whose width corresponded to that of the still existing pronaos) we are led to think that the front which the Roman architect had planned for the Theatine church was developed on two orders. They were animated by chiaroscuro effects of four niches and with four pilaster strips for each order, with Corinthian capitals on one order and composite on the other, and a large window with a triangular tympanum over the door-way.

The still-existing pronaos could not but imply a triangular tympanum and the «frontespizio» with the two «sexangule» windows according to a solution which will later be adopted by the same architect, in the first order of the front of the chapel of *Monte di Pietà*.

In the meantime, the decoration of the whole nave continued[31] and between 1590 and 1591 Cavagna, together with Tommaso Maurizio, worked there as a painter too[32].

In 1592 the XVI century nave was completed and it is possible to infer a complete description of it — corresponding to its actual architectonic aspect — from the stucco-workers' payments. We can note marked transvers pilasters, typical of the rhytmic truss (Albertiano), which makes the curve leitmotif dominant throughout the succession of high and low arches. It should be noted, however, that the six windows, in addition to the large one in the rear wall, (made by Giovanni Smelleres only in correspondance to the highest arches) show that the longitudinal development the internal space had at that time terminated in correspondance to the penultimate arcade.

On the 19th October 1603, Giovambattista del Tufo consecrated the church though it had not yet been completely finished[33]. As a matter of fact, the work was suspended for several years, until 1627 when «i Padri volsero fare l'ale nella chiesa e anche allongarla alla sua bona proportione...»[34]. The aisles and the extension of the nave must have been built between 1626 and 1630[35]. A new architect, Giovan Giacomo di Conforto[36], worked on the construction from 28th February 1626 till the end of 1627. He had carried out several plans by F. Grimaldi and from 1615 onwards he had been engaged in the work in *S.S. Trinità delle Monache*. Between 1627 and 1630 he also directed the building of the churches of *S.S. Apostoli* and *S. Maria della Sapienza*.

The fact that di Conforto had worked on the construction of *S. Paolo* during these years, when the aisles were being built, could enhance the hypothesis that he was the author of the plan of *S. Paolo* and that the drawings by Cavagna for the nave were variations of a previous plan.

The architectonic idea of aisles with successively small chapels is similar to the structure of *S. Maria degli Angeli a Pizzofalcone*, in Naples, planned by Grimaldi as well; but in *S. Paolo* it is realized with great originality, in a succession of small elliptical cupolas and vaults with fanlights. As in the church of *SS. Apostoli* here too di Conforto, probably modifies the classicism of Grimaldi's language with his own, aimed at creating dynamic spaces. In this case he succeeds in doing so by changing the previous plan that probably implied a succession of small spherical vaults.

We can presume that Cavagna did the same, modifing an original plan by introducing the rhythmic truss, later adopted by G.G. di Conforto in almost all his work[37].

This is mere hypothesis since we do not know any of Cavagna's religious edifices save the church of *S. Gregorio Armeno*. In the structure of the single aisle we are reminded of the church of *Gesù* by Vignola.

After having worked as an architect and painter in *S. Paolo Maggiore*, Cavagna remained in Naples, where some years later, he took upon himself the task of his most ambitious work, the construction of the *Monte di Pietà*.

As an institution the *Monte di Pietà* has its origin in an attempt to defeat usury by a social and economic promise, giving loans in pawn with no interest.

Façade of the Building, «Roman» balcony, first floor

Entrance-hall of the Building

Between the end of the XII and the XIV centuries[38] the first three pawnshops were founded in Northern Europe, but they had short lives owing to a lack of funds and proper organization.

A wider diffusion of these institutions took place thanks to some Franciscan Friars intent upon defeating the usury practiced at that time by Hebrews and «Caorsini». Thus Fra' Barnaba da Terni, in 1462 established the *Monte di Pietà* in Perugia, obtaining the money necessary to open the pawnshop through alms[39]. During the XVI century Naples too had its *Monte di Pietà* thanks to Aurelio Paparo and Leonardo di Palma[40]. In 1539 i.e. a year before the banishment of Hebrews from the reign, at the wish of Pedro de Toledo, they transferred all that the citizen had pawned to their house in *Selice* Street near the *Giudecca*, beginning there the practice of lending money without interest[41]; the *Monte* was then transferred to the *Casa Santa dell'Annunziata* where it survived for over twenty years[42].

Legacies, born as a consequence of the Counter-reformation doctrine of the salvation of the soul through charity, not only contributed to the enrichment and development of convents, but also determined the creation of several religious institutions such as seminaries, brotherhoods, academies of music, congregations, schools, hospitals and so on. The *Monte di Pietà* too was enriched by gifts and legacies, and by a greater number of pledges. It soon appeared as an institution with new and broader banking functions, officially acknowledged in 1584, by a public recognition signed by the viceroy Duke d'Ossuna[43]. The original seat no longer answered to the new exigencies and it became necessary to take larger quarters, thus the palace of the Dukes d'Andria Carafa, in *Largo S. Marcellino*, was rented for six hundred ducats a year[44].

As soon as, in 1576, 171071,71 ducats of capital[45] were achieved, the patrons Cesare Miroballo, Alfonso Gaetano, Camillo Macedonio, Paolo Balzerano, Ferrante Imparato and Giovan Tommaso Borrelli bought the D. Girolamo Carafa's palace, located in the *Nilo* district[46], from Delizia Gesualdo, mother and guardian of the young Francesco Carafa, for 16.300 ducats.

The palace was completely rebuilt, the plan being given to G.B. Cavagna, who personally directed the new construction remarkable, among other things, for the functional quality responding to particular needs, requiring far different solutions as compared to other public buildings.

This aspect was soon emphasized by G.C. Capaccio. He writes: «...si vede fabbricato con ogni comodità per ricever e consegnar pegni, sontuosissimo nell'apparato di panni, sete, tele, tapezzerie...»[47], followed by C. Celano, according to whom «...l'architetto devesi lodare di sommo giudizio, perché oltre alla divisione così ben'intesa dei luoghi ed officine, oltre a non esservi un palmo di terra infruttuosa, disegnò la casa, non solo per l'opera che era in quel tempo ma per l'accrescimento che poteva avere...»[48]; according to B. De Dominici «...ideò un disegno, che fosse con magnificenza diviso ogni sito di officio e con sommo giudizio dato il comodo a tutti»[49].

In the *Banco di Napoli* historical archives we can see the *Libri di Casa* of the *Monte di Pietà* where all the payments to those who worked for the realization of the new building are recorded in detail. In addition to Cavagna, recurring names of the architectonic history of Naples in XVI and XVII

Entrance-hall of the Building. The façade of the Chapel can be seen on the background of the court-yard centuries are recorded: Giovan Giacomo di Conforto e Giovan Cola di Franco, both active «in solidum» in the construction with no interruption till 1603, when on the 3rd January we read: «... E più duc. 6.5 a GG. di Conforto e Gio. Cola di Franco fabricatori per saldo de residui e giornate sino al 4 del presente»[50]; Ceccardo Bernucci and Cristoforo Monterosso, «marmorari», who since 11th July 1598 had been receiving 100 ducats «...in conto di marmi di carrara di massa e di caserta, ch'insolidum prometteno far venire a loro spese a la fabrica del Monte e lavorarli conforme al ordine se li darà da Gio. Battista Cavagni incigniero di quella, per la cappella e porta del palazzo e per la lumaca, da starsi a gioditio del signor Marchese di Grottola o d'altri...»[51]; Vito Alfieri, who is recorded as «soprastante» in the new construction till the 16th December 1602 when he received his last salary, having requested and obtained from the governors to be dismissed from that duty[52].

It is possible to infer from this detailed documents that Cavagna not only made the plan of the building, but he directly and constantly intervened during its construction and decoration, at least until the first months of 1603, personally attending at the stucco and gilding of the chapel, as well.

On 14 February 1598 G.B. Cavagna «incigniero» was paid 85 ducats «a compimento di ducati cento per saldo di tutte le fatiche e servitù fatti nel far deli disegni per la Casa nova del Monte, et altre cose per detta fabrica, per tutto gennaro 1598, che li restanti docati 15 li hebbe contanti, come appare da un libretto di spese dichiarando, che dal primo di febraro avante li fu stabilita provisione di docati 12 il mese dorante la detta fabrica, così ordinato in congregatione a 12 di questo...»[53]. In fact, beginning in February 1598, a monthly salary of twelve ducats was paid to Cavagna as construction engineer: «...duc. 12 a Gio. Batta Cavagni, per la sua mesata di febraro 98, stabiliti da signori protettori in congregazione a 17 de febraro per l'officio d'incigniero, e cura, che lui tiene de la fabrica»[54]. Cavagna received this monthly payment till June 1602 and though in the *Libri di Casa* no further payments to Cavagna result after that date, he nevertheless continued to be interested in the works of the *Monte di Pietà* building, by supervising the duties of the various masters or by making ascertainments together with other architects[55].

We shall attempt to review the course of the work by citing the most significant documents in our possession.

On 14 Febraury 1598 G.B. Cavagna received 85 ducats to settle the entire sum of 100 ducats for the plans of the new building of the *Monte di Pietà*. A wooden model of the whole plan was made by Francesco De Simone, who on 24 April, received the last six ducats of the 76 ducats agreed upon[56]. In 1598 the first stone of the chapel was laid; on September of the same year, in fact, a payment is recorded: «...ducati 4.10 a Vincenzo Buonocore spesi in mortelle, et altro nela venuta del Rev.mo Cardinal Gisualdo a buttar la nova pietra nele pedamenta de la cappella della nova casa del monte...»[57]. On June 1600, the rough structure of the palace must have been terminated as: «Gio. Batta Cavagni vadi dal Marchese di Grottola per aver resolutione delli cornicione che s'ha da fare dentro lo cortile della casa nuova si de pietre di Sorrento, ò di stucco»[58] and on February 1601 we read «... a di 26... duc. 6 pagati a Gio. Battista Caracciolo per la pittura di chiar'oscuro fatto a fresco de li sei puttini al frontespizio del muro de la cappella del novo monte...»[59]. On 28 June 1602 payments were made of: «... duc. 60: 1.7 ... a ber.no Vassallo a compimento di duc. 275.1.7 per saldo dell'opra del stucco fatta nella cappella del banco, e tre camare de la congregatione come per lista de Cavagni incigniero infilata...»[60]; in 1603 the work was practically completed and Giovan Giacomo di Conforto and Giovan Cola di Franco «fabricatori», received final settlement for their work and, on 17 January «... stante la relatione dell'architetto Gio. Battista Cavagni se paghino ducati 55 a Gioseppe Mellone a compimento dei ducati 100 per conto della indoratura della cappella»[61]; the following month «... duc. 15 a compimento di ducati trenta in conto de rigiole per la cappella conforme al disegno di Cavagni»[62]; were paid and finally in May of the same year Giacomo was paid 3 ducats «... per la fattura del modello de legno delorologio»[63].

The ashlar-work seen on the first order of the front of *S. Gregorio Armeno*, appears extended on the façade of the palace, with a preponderance of chiaroscuro effects in respect of the pilaster delimitating external spaces and the large portal.

Moreover, Cavagna was inspired by XVI century Neapolitan buildings which, as a consequence of the narrow spaces in front of them, have greater window-openings on the second instead of the first floor in order to allow better lightning: as a matter of fact he planned the five balconies «alla romana» on the second floor: the three central ones corresponding to a hall and the other two, on the two sides, corresponding to stairs. They are surmounted by alternate circular and triangular tympanums with the impost frame interrupted by a bas-relief with the symbol of the *Monte di Pietà*. The top floor presents squared windows having only slightly projecting bands in order to emphasize the lower tympanums: the last floor is delimited upward by a frame with corbels and rose-windows, that can be found also inside the building around the whole perimeter of the court which after a brief interruption, continues on the lesser façades in a more simplified manner with no rose-windows. Monumental as it is, the palace, was defined by F. Milizia «un bel pezzo di architettura»[64].

It recalls some of Della Porta's motifs. It has its finest expression in the great hall where the median arch scenographically frames the front of the chapel located in the rear of the court.

The space of the hall is divided in depth by four pilasters joined to the perimetral walls by round arches and ribbed vaults.

The chapel is undoubtedly the predominant element of the court; it was built at the same time as the palace and its first stone, blessed by Cardinal Alfonso Gesualdo, archibishop of Naples, was laid in the presence of viceroy Enrico de Gusman, Count of Olivares[65]. On that occasion, there was some disagreement between laical and ecclesiastical authorities about the name to be engraved on the first stone: the laical power won since instead of the name of the Pope, it was engraved the symbol of the *Monte di Pietà*, the royal crown and the croos on one side and the inscription «Philippo Rege» on the other[66].

The internal walls and the vaults of the single aisle are completely covered by painted marble and gold stuccos. The rather small aisle presents lacunars of different shapes that do not alter the distribution of the ceiling: on the

The Building court-yard.
The Building court-yard. The adjoining walls presenting windows of two different types

contrary they underline the three points of the vault, among which the central cross-vault and the following ones, along the perimeter of the chapel, characterized by alternate arches and pilasters. In correspondance to the presbitery there are three altars and on the minor points of the side walls the marble balustrades of the high small choirs jut out supported by corbels. The front is emphasized by four Jonic pilaster strips made of bardiglio marble which delimitate two lateral spaces — containing two niches with the statues of *Carità* and *Sicurezza* by Pietro Bernini — and a wider central one displaying a fine portal in red marble surmounted by a window.

The employment of difficult materials give an intense chromatic effect to the whole, while the plastic scanning is stressed by the white marble of the capitals, the scroll ornaments and the frieze which reads: «O Magnum Pietatis Opus».

The front terminates with a triangular tympanum holding the high-relief of the *Deposizione*, by Michelangelo Naccherino which breaks the harmonious integration of architecture and sculpture characterizing the whole front, ill arranged with respect to the background and invading most of the frame. On the contrary, the wall above the chapel is well conceived: one part of it is an attic, accented by simple panels that call our attention to the rich window framing of the niche of the clock[67] which completes the scene between two small pinnacles.

According to B. Molajoli, the chiaroscuro, frescoes (today completely faded) which filled the backgrounds of the upper panels «...non assolvono più alla loro funzione coloristica originaria d'annullamento della massa di superficie e quindi in funzione della maggiore unità chiaroscurale dell'insieme, in coordinamento con la zona inferiore spezzata dalla varietà dei marmi delle statue e delle cartelle»[68].

The harmony of the neat, organic distribution of decorative elements in the court is broken by a wing which corresponds to the arches of the hall: even if it repeats the same distribution of lights of the external façade, in the lower order, it is clearly incomplete, evidenced by the two big corbels corresponding to the central arch probably meant to support a balustrade of a balcony, as the sudden interruption of the parastas flanked by the flat vaults. Moreover, there is no link between the arches and the adjoining walls, that, on the groundfloor, present the same motif as the door with the window on the front of the chapel, though less elaborate. This lack of continuity is partly due to the enormous size of the pilasters, probably intended to allow a view of the entire court, even from the entrance[69].

In the same years of construction of the palace of the *Monte di Pietà* the bank of *S. Maria del Popolo* was being built, opened by the *Ospedale degli Incurabili* which was established in the first half of XVI century by Maria Longo, who devoted herself to treating those who suffered from serious illnesses[70]. As soon as she depleted her personal economic resources, and wishing to continue her charitable work, Maria Longo began to beg for alms from whomever came to visit the patients. She collected money enough to carry on with her work and also to help those prostitutes who wished to redeem themselves. She then founded three monasteries for them: the *Conventuali* for those who wanted to take care of sick patients, the *Riformate* for those who took their monastic

Façade of the Chapel, portal

Façade of the Chapel, portal, decorative detail

vows and the *Cappuccinelle* or *Trentatré*, the one with the strictest rules[71].
Here Maria Longo spent the last years of her life after having left to Maria
Aierbo, Duchess of Termoli, the task of continuing her work. When the latter
died, the administration of the hospital and of the monasteries was devolved
on a council of noblemen of the reign[72].
In 1582, two Neapolitan merchants, Corcione and Composta, opened a bank
named *Incurabiles* and gave part of the revenues to the hononymous hospital.
This enterprise, which lasted only a few years, and the example of the
Annunziata, led the governors of the hospital to set up a Bank both for
circulation and deposit, calling it *S. Maria del Popolo*[73].
Owing to its increasing turnover, larger headquarters were needed and, in
1597, the Bank was transferred to a building in *S. Lorenzo* street[74], later
enlarged thanks to the purchase of some houses by Ludamia Morello and the
Mazzacane sisters as well as the renting of some premises owned by the
convent of *S. Gregorio Armeno*[75].
Documentary sources disclose that the governors of the *Incurabili* wished to
demolish the old houses, including the ones they had rented from the convent
of *S. Gregorio Armeno* in order to build a new and larger building, more
suitable to the needs of the Bank.
In the register of the notary Giovan Battista Basso we can read the agreement
stipulated on 8 November 1597 with the builders Giovan Andrea and Cesare
Quaranta who «prometteno fare tutta la fabrica bona et perfetta a laude et
giuditio all'ingegniero deputando e secondo il designo che li serré ordinato per
detto ingegniero...»[76].
Thus the architect of the new building had not yet been appointed. Yet on
the *Giornali di cassa* of the Bank of *S. Maria del Popolo*, on June 1598 we read
«...Al nostro Banco conto di fabrica ducati 10 e per lui e per la casa santa a
Gio.batta Cavagna per alcuni serviti et disegni che ha fatto per la nuova
fabrica che si fa alle Case site ad San Lorenzo et altro per servitio di detta
Casa Santa»[77].
There is no information, neither here nor elsewhere, as to which drawings
were intended, neverthless it seems that G.B. Cavagna was simultaneously
engaged in the building of the *Monte di Pietà* and in the building of the Bank
of *S. Maria del Popolo*. Today this building is practically non-existent; the front
on *Tribunali* street and on the adjacent square of *S. Lorenzo* has been
completely changed, embodying, the altered XVI century structure and
preserving the ancient «piperno» portal, while the façade near *S. Gregorio
Armeno* monastery is timeworn and crumbling[78]. Only the first order survives,
very probably including the main entrance of the Bank.
The «piperno» framework on a background of bricks enclosed by light
marble squares creates a subtle chromatic effect.
The plan of distribution is quite similar to the façade of the *Monte di Pietà*,
displaying, however, motifs drawn from *S. Gregorio Armeno* in the treatment
of the embossed portal.
Eight embossed pilaster strips highlight the wall, the four central ones being
thick while the lateral ones are thinner.
The succession of vertical elements is interrupted by a high «fascia» that
resembles an attic, on which a triangular tympanum dominates the portal,

Interior of the Chapel

while the parastas are completely smooth and are culminated by a pedestal supporting a globe.

What remains of the façade of the bank of *S. Maria del Popolo* is like the *Monte di Pietà* the expression of a language no longer limited by local taste, but inspired by more learned models. The still existing decorative details, such as the powerful proportions of the framework, the combination of «piperno» and bricks, the notable tympanum, the fascia resembling an attic, are all solutions, similar to those adopted by D. Fontana for the royal palace.

In a bitterly polemical manuscript against D. Fontana[79] we read that Cavagna, while assisting in the construction of the *Monte di Pietà*, was also working on a plan for a new royal palace.

The refusal of his plan probably induced the artist to leave the court and settle in Loreto where, in 1605, he succeeded Muzio Oddi in the construction of the *Santa Casa*[80] and where he died in July 1413.

[1] For what concerns the origins of the Catholic-Tridentine reform in Naples and the consequences of its application cnf. *Le origini della riforma cattolica-tridentina a Napoli*, in *Problemi di vita religiosa in Italia nel Cinquecento*, Padova, 1960, pp. 317 foll.; P. LOPEZ, *Riforma cattolica e vita religiosa e culturale a Napoli dalla fine del '500 ai primi del '700*, Napoli, 1964, pp. 1-16; J. MAZZOLENI, *Aspetti della riforma cattolica e del concilio di Trento a Napoli*, ivi, 1956; H. JEDIN, *Riforma cattolica e Controriforma*, in AA.VV., «Storia della Chiesa», Milano, 1975, pp. 518 foll.

[2] F. NICOLINI, *Aspetti della vita italo-spagnola del Cinque e Seicento*, Napoli, 1934, p. 310.

[3] In this regard cnf. P. GIANNONE, *Historia civile del regno di Napoli*, ivi, 1723, vol. XXXVIII, chap. V., para. I and F. STRAZZULLO, *Edilizia e urbanistica a Napoli dal '500 al '700*, Napoli, 1968, pp. 79 foll.; see also G.C. ALISIO, *Sviluppo urbano e struttura della città*, in «Storia di Napoli», ivi, 1971, vol. VIII, pp. 314 foll.

[4] R. PANE, *Il monastero napoletano di S. Gregorio Armeno*, Napoli, 1957, pp. 47 foll., and by the same author, *Monasteri napoletani del centro antico*, in «Napoli nobilissima», II (1963), p. 203.

[5] A. VENDITTI, *Fra' Nuvolo e l'architettura napoletana tra Cinque e Seicento*, in «Barocco europeo, barocco italiano, barocco salentino», Atti del congresso internazionale sul Barocco, Lecce 21-24 September 1969, pp. 54-56; M. ROTILI, *L'arte del Cinquecento nel regno di Napoli*, ivi, 1972, pp. 82-87.

[6] The artist died in Loreto and his remains were buried in the town cathedral on 19th July 1613 (cnf. P. GIANNIZZI, *Rassegna bibliografica dell'arte italiana*, IX (1906), p. 163).

[7] A. BERTOLOTTI, *Artisti lombardi a Roma nei secoli XV-XVI-XVII*, Milano, 1881, I, p. 125.

[8] The *retablo mayor* of the monastery of *Santa Maria della Vid*, sent to Spain by the viceroy Juan de Zuniga in the years 1591-92, contains a *Presentazione al tempio* of 1591 signed G.B. CAVAGNA (cnf. G. PREVITALI, *La pittura del Cinquecento a Napoli e nel Vicereame*, Torino, 1978, p. 110).

[9] G.B. D'ADDOSIO, *Documenti inediti di artisti napoletani dei secoli XVI e XVII dalle polizze dei Banchi*, in «Archivio storico per le province napoletane», XXXVIII (1913), pp. 41 e 42; ivi, XLIV (1919), p. 384; G. BRESCIANO, *Documenti inediti concernenti artisti napoletani del Quattro e Cinquecento*, in «A.S.P.N.», LII (1927), pp. 369-370; G. SOBOKTA, *ad vocem*, U. THIEME - F. BECKER, *Allegemeines Lexicon der bildenden künstler*, Leipzig, 1907 foll., vol. VI, p. 211.

[10] R. PANE, *Il monastero napoletano*, op. cit.; F. STRAZZULLO, *Architetti e ingegneri napoletani dal '500 al '700*, Napoli, 1959, pp. 98-114.

[11] Benedictine archive of S. Gregorio Armeno, *Libro d'introito ed esito*, 1568-1569, pp. 136 and 136v in A. D'ESPOSITO, *Giovan Battista Cavagna, architetto romano a Napoli*, dissertation on History of Architecture, Faculty of Literature and Philosophy, University of Naples, academical year 1985-86. See also historical archive of Naples, «notaio» G.B. Pacifico, 12 Luglio 1572, in D'Esposito, op. cit..

[12] From the document published by F. STRAZZULLO, (*Architetti e ingegneri...*, op. cit., p. 108) concerning the agreement between Della Monica and the Benedictine nuns of S. Marcellino about the new construction of their monastery, we may clearly infer that Della Monica merely executed a plan made by someone else. Strazzullo recalls that the clauses concerning the acceptance of the contract work were signed by the abess, V. Della Monica and others, among which Giovan Francesco Di Palma who died before September 1572 (F. STRAZZULLO, *Architetti e ingegneri...*, op. cit., p. 299) i.e. in the period between the signing of the contract and the beginning of the works in October of the same year.

[13] His presence is supported by documents dating from 24 February 1581 to 29 May 1583 («Accademia Nazionale di San Luca, Archivio Storico», *Libro dei pagamenti*, vol. 41, pp. 18v, 19v, 88v, 91, 92v, 93 in D'ESPOSITO, op. cit.).

[14] *Archivio di Stato di Napoli, Monasteri Soppressi*; (from now on A.S.N., Mon. Soppr.), vol. 1071, p. 3.

[15] B. DI FALCO, *Descrittione dei luoghi antiqui di Napoli*, Edited by O. Morisani, Napoli 1972, p. 44.

[16] A.S.N., Mon. Soppr., vol. 1071, p. 7; in this regard cnf. R. CORRERA, «Il tempio dei Dioscuri», in *Atti della R. Acc. di Arch., Lett. e B.A.*, XIII (1905), p. 216.

[17] S. SAVARESE, *Francesco Grimaldi e l'architettura della Controriforma a Napoli*, Roma, 1986, pp. 54-55.

[18] A.S.N., Mon. Soppr., vol. 1131, p. 93.

[19] Ivi, vol. 1131, p. 109 v.

[20] Ivi, vol. 1131, p. 91.

[21] Ivi, vol. 1131, p. 81.

[22] Ivi, vol. 1131, p. 109.

[23] A.S.N., Mon. Soppr., vol. 1131, f. 134.

[24] D'ANCORA, ms. XXVII D 6, fasc. XIII, n. 7 at the Società di Storia Patria di Napoli.

[25] A. QUATTRONE, *P.D. Francesco Grimaldi C.R. Architetto*, in «Regnum Dei», V (1949), p. 43. Hibbard agrees with Quattrone in: *The early history of Sant'Andrea della Valle*, in «The Art Bullettin», XLIII (1961), p. 302.

[26] F. CEVA GRIMALDI, *Memorie storiche della città di Napoli dal tempo della sua fondazione sino al presente*, Napoli, 1857, p. 370.

[27] A.S.N., Mon. Soppr., vol. 1131, p. 148.

[28] Ivi, vol. 1131, p. 150. These documents, already published by Carrera (op. cit., p. 217) led him and L. Serra (*Note sullo svolgimento dell'architettura barocca a Napoli*, in *Nap. nob.*, II n.s. (1921), pp. 88-89), to ascribe the whole plan of transformation of the medieval basilica to G.B. Cavagna.

[29] A. Bulifon, *Giornali di Napoli dal 1547 al 1706*, edited by N. Cortese, Napoli, 1932, vol. I, p. 63.

[30] A.S.N., Mon. Soppr., vol. 1131, pp. 154-154v, 164.

[31] Ivi, vol. 1131, pp. 158, 165-165v.

[32] Ivi, vol. 1131, pp. 114v, 115, 162 e 164.

[33] C. D'Engenio Caracciolo, *Napoli Sacra*, Napoli, 1624, p. 86.

[34] V. Pagano, *Breve relazione del principio e progressi della religione dei chierici regolari e delle attioni d'alcuni di essi padri*, sec. XVII, ms. 564 of the Fondo S. Martino in the Biblioteca Nazionale di Napoli, p. 117.

[35] A.S.N., Mon. Soppr., vol. 1179, f. 49.

[36] As a matter of fact, in the documents of the convent we may find from 28 February 1626 onwards some payments to «Gio. Jacono Conforto architetto per le sue fatiche» (A.S.N., Mon. soppr., vol. 1179, p. 55). Other payments are recorded: 9 May and 1[rst] October of the same year and in January, June and September of the following year (cnf. pp. 56-70).

[37] For a more detailed analysis of events concerning the lengthy period of construction of the church of S. Paolo Maggiore cnf. Savarese, op. cit., pp. 48-69.

[38] Cnf. E. Tortora, *Nuovi documenti per la storia del Banco di Napoli*, ivi, 1890, p. 11.

[39] Ivi, p. 12.

[40] According to some scholars (cnf. M. Rocco, *Dei banchi di Napoli e della loro ragione*, Napoli, 1785-87, vol. I, p. 151) the *Monte di Pietà* in Naples was founded by the viceroy Pedro de Toledo in 1540 after the ban of the Hebrews from the reign. Tortora disagrees with this theory on the basis of demonstrative documents of the Banco.

[41] Rocco, op. cit., p. 152.

[42] Tortora, op. cit., p. 17.

[43] B. Molajoli, *Opere d'arte del Banco di Napoli. La cappella del Monte di Pietà. La galleria d'arte*, Napoli 1953, p. 12.

[44] Tortora, op. cit., p. 34.

[45] Ivi, p. 35.

[46] Archivio Storico del Banco di Napoli (from this date forward A.S.B.N.), *Libro di Casa*, matr. 184 «E» 1597-1602. All the documentation concerning the *Monte di Pietà* building and the *Banco di S. Maria del Popolo* has been taken from D. Esposito, op. cit., after careful verification.

[47] G.C. Capaccio, *Il forastiero*, Napoli, 1634, p. 918.

[48] C. Celano, *Notizie del bello, dell'antico e del curioso della città di Napoli* etc., ivi, 1692, vol. III, p. 728.

[49] B. De Dominici, *Vite di pittori, scultori e architetti napoletani*, Napoli, 1742-45, vol. III, p. 172.

[50] A.S.B.N., *Libro di Casa...* cit., 3 January 1603.

[51] Ivi, 11 July 1598.

[52] Ivi, 16 December 1602.

[53] Ivi, 14 February 1598.

[54] Ivi, 2 March 1598.

[55] Ivi, 28 June 1602: «Et a di detto... duc. 60: I-7 pagati a ber.no Vassallo a compimento di duc. 275.I.7 per saldo dell'opra del stucco fatta ne la cappella banco, e tre camare de la congregatione come per lista de Cavagni incigniero infilata...»; ivi, 31 July 1602: «...duc. 4 pagati a Gio. Batta Cavagno incigniero, Col'Antonio Angelosa, Pignalosa Cafaro e Costantino Avallone pro eguali parte, per accesso e consulta data che si levi lo stipo fatto in la sala e si ponghi la guardarobba del monte»; ivi, 30 October 1602: «Et a di detto ducati otto pagati a Gioseppo Cristiano per relatione di Gio. batta Cavagni per lo stucco e lavore di quello posto nel arco de la guadarobba deloro...»; ivi, 28 November 1602: «... duc. 80 pagati a Costantino Avallone e Gio. batta Cavagni, cio è duc. 40 per ciascuno per loro fatiche fatte in misurar la casa del monte...».

[56] A.S.B.N., *Libro di Casa...* cit., 24 April 1599.

[57] Ivi, 20 September 1598.

[58] A.S.B.N., *Libro di conclusioni del Monte di Pietà*, 1600-1602, 26 June 1600.

[59] A.S.B.N., *Libro di Casa...* cit., 26 February 1601.

[60] Ivi, 28 June 1602.

[61] A.S.B.N., *Libro di conclusioni...* cit., 17 January 1603.

[62] A.S.B.N., *Libro di Casa...* cit., 4 February 1603.

[63] Ivi, 28 May 1603.

[64] F. Milizia, *Dizionario delle Belle Arti del disegno*, Bassano, 1822, p. 184.

[65] M. Morelli - L. Conforti, *La cappella del Monte di Pietà*, Napoli, 1899, pp. 15-16.

[66] C. Coniglio, *I viceré spagnoli di Napoli*, ivi, 1967, p. 55.

[67] B. Molajoli (op. cit., p. 15) refers that: «un disegno de cartone per vedere s'è bene far ponere l'horologio sopra il frontespizio della cappella» was ordered too.

[68] ibidem.

[69] R. Pane, *Architettura dell'età barocca a Napoli*, ivi, 1939, p. 33.

[70] Tortora, *Nuovi documenti...* cit., p. 65-66.

[71] Ivi, p. 68.

[72] Ibidem.

[73] Ibidem.

[74] A.S.B.N., Banco di S. Maria del Popolo, *Giornali di Banco*, matr. 25, 1600, 11 August, Friday: the *Banco* is in the «...casa e botteghe site alla strada di S. Lorenzo... dalli 22 di ottobre 1597...».

[75] TORTORA, op. cit., p. 74.

[76] A.S.N., notaio G.B. Basso, 1597-1598, p. 110.

[77] A.S.B.N., Banco di S. Maria del Popolo, *Giornali di cassa*, matr. 17, 9 June 1598.

[78] A survey together with a plan of the building of the *Banco* executed by Pietro Vinaccia on 13 May 1747 is still existent (A.S.N., Mon. Soppr., vol. 3430).

[79] The manuscript was published by A. MIOLA, Cavagna contro Fontana a proposito della reggia di Napoli, in «Nap. nob.» I, 1892), pp. 89-91 and 99-103 and by F. STRAZZULLO, *Architetti e ingegneri...* cit., pp. 75 foll.

[80] R. PANE, *Architettura dell'età barocca...* cit., p. 33.

The Pictoral Cycle and the Sacred Furniture
by Fausta Navarro

Criticism about Corenzio

«Che che ne sia del suo costume, convien fare giustizia al vero, e dire che Belisario in varie chiese ha dipinto istoriette di picciole figure, così ben condotte, che meritano attenzione e lode da gl'intendenti; dappoiché vi si scorge uno spirito ed un gusto del colore, che manca a molti suoi componimenti, come può vedersi nella cappella, o sia chiesuola eretta nel cortile del Sacro Monte della Pietà; ove in molti compartimenti di stucco dorato egli figurò Misteri della Vita del nostro Redentore, così dolorosi come gloriosi e vi sono figure bellissime in disegno, azione e componimento, con buone piegature di panni, che veramente, come dissi, son degne di lode; e massimamente le figure solitarie, che son dipinte né compartimenti di quelle istorie, alcune delle quali rappresentano Profeti e Santi, che sono bellissime; e questa Cappella vien lodata da' professori come una delle opere migliori di Bellisario; essendo che ella è dipinta con studio e grande armonia di colori...».
With these words the Neapolitan historian Bernardo De Dominici expresses his opinion of Corenzio, commenting on the frescoes in the *Monte di Pietà* a century and a half after their completion[1].
The conclusions are undeniably positive. Not only does De Dominici manifest his appreciation of the work but he evaluates the characteristics of Corenzio's style with fine philological discernment, e.g. "lo spirito, il gusto e la grande armonia del colore". In other, more modern terms, the ability to enliven a vivid and expressive scene through the use of a range of pale colours melting into the atmosphere.
The 17th century historian substantially anticipates the judgments expressed about Corenzio by the most knowledgeable critics, revealing an acute sensibility in his understanding of works of art — despite the anti-mannerist prejudices springing from his academic ideals[2]. The fame of being an envious and wicked man weighs heavily on Belisario Corenzio, apparently ready to resort to any means — even to the actual physical elimination of his rivals — in order to determine his victory in professional competitions[3]. De Dominici consolidates and advances this fame, committing Corenzio to posterity as the leader — together with Ribera and Battistello Caracciolo — of the Neapolitan artistic camorra[4]. Nevertheless, De Dominici is ready to recognize in Corenzio his inexhaustible abilities as a fresco painter and decorator, indicating, in his works, a starting-point and illustrious example to the local fresco artists who, a century later, were to be protagonists of the imposing epoch of Neapolitan baroque: «gli si deve rendere onore per tutte quelle parti di che inanzi si è ragionato, e per aver aperto una strada facile all'inventare, ammirandosi fra le sue figura positure difficili, ma fatte con disinvoltura, e con faciltà spiegata quell'azione...»[5].
Towards the close of the century Luigi Lanzi quite faithfully recaptures the judgment of De Dominici. In particular, complete credit was given to the affirmation that the artist had spent five years in the workshop of Tintoretto, in Venice. Lanzi considers Corenzio as a painter rich in inventive powers and nimble in his execution. The critic becomes more original when he affirms that «Corenzio tenne spesso una maniera in molte cose conforme allo stile del Cavalier d'Arpino» and that he carefully considers the Venetian painters[6].

Contemporary philologists have confirmed and developed these critical judgments[7].

Neapolitan guidebooks are rather lacking in information concerning the decorations in the *Monte di Pietà* and, in general, the other decorative works by Corenzio[8].

At the end of the 18th century Sigismondo mentions the frescoed decorations done by the painter in the rooms of the *Officine*, the bank of the *Monte di Pietà* and in the church, making incidental reference to the paintings by Borghese and Santafede[9]. In a somewhat more detailed fashion Chiarini speaks of the «maggior robustezza di pennello», while in the paintings on canvas he admires «il bell'effetto di chiaroscuro, gl'ingegnosi e difficili scorci, la naturalezza dei colori»[10].

The phase of acquisition of documentary evidence concerning Corenzio dates from 1873 to 1919 without, however, any attempt to reconstruct the artistic personality of the artist. The lengthy series of documents relating to payments for cycles of frescoes in the principal Neapolitan churches — and no lack of information about paintings for private individuals[11] — confirm the enormous number of works accomplished by the painter, and already recorded by De Dominici[12]. The most voluminous publications of documents are attributable to Faraglia in the magazine *Archivio Storico delle Provincie Napoletane*, to Ceci and Colombo in *Napoli Nobilissima* and to D'Addosio, again in the *Archivio Storico delle Provincie Napoletane*[13].

At the beginning of the 20th century we see the first critical treatment — by scholars such as Rolfs and Sobotka — intent, above all, in preparing a rational catalogue of the works of Corenzio, outlining his artistic personality within the general frame of late-Manneristic Neapolitan painting. We are dealing here with true pioneering in the almost unexplored field of Neapolitan painting[14]. From the postwar period on, however, with the development of a strain of specialized artistic literature on the subject, as well as the consequent reappraisal of Southern Italian Mannerism, the artistic spirit of Belisario has been the object of renewed investigations[15]. In particular, the studies of Giovanni Previtali, from 1972 to the present day, and those of Walter Witzthum in the field of drawing, have consented to an inedited clarification of the figure of Belisario Corenzio and thrown new light on many aspects of his work. Following a reliable chronology, Previtali has carried out his studies in a climate of renewed and careful research into the Neapolitan artistic atmosphere of the last twenty years of that century — the years which saw an affirmation in Naples of the «maniera dolce e pastosa» (soft and mellow manner) of Taddeo and Federico Zuccari and the international Mannerism with roots in the neo-Parma school, as well as the baroque current. In Belisario's work all these aspects blend together, giving life to light-hearted and spirited painting, decorative and highly successful[16].

Vitzthum has taken into consideration part of the vast array of graphic material, providing an initial reorganization based on characteristics of style; he has further placed in the proper light the superior quality and the extremely personal manner revealed in the drawings of Corenzio. This rearrangement, interrupted by the untimely death of the scholar, is, however, far from being completed[17].

At the present time we can only say that the first steps have been taken for a reconstruction of the artistic personality of Belisario Corenzio, today more renowned than known.

Imagery of the Frescoes in the «Monte di Pietà»

The iconographic intent of the decorations and frescoes as well as the façade of the chapel in the *Monte di Pietà* were inspired by the clients[18].
We learn, in fact, that on 19th August 1602 the Protectorate of the *Monte di Pietà* handed over to Belisario Corenzio «la lista de li Misteri della Passione» to represent on the vault of the chapel[19]. The theme of the Passion of Jesus Christ was particularly dear to the Church of the Counter-Reformation since it expressed one of the cardinal dogmas of the faith and was, at the same time, a strong stimulus to Christian piety. We have no precise information concerning the iconographic choices of the Protectors for the frescoes in the Congregation Room and the Bank but we can hazard a guess about their intervention here, too — all the more so as these rooms were destined for a public function. For the most part the frescoes represent allegories of Virtue, undoubtedly chosen by the administrators of the *Monte* for their analogy with the charitable goal of the institution. Or else, as in the case of the figure in the first room — a woman with a flowering shrub and the terrestrial globe in her hands, symbolizing the allegory of an activity, agriculture, denoting work of the earth — which could well be compared with the work of the *Monte*[20]. And it is this activity — summarized in the motto of the inscription «Condita conservare meum est» that prompts the fruit offered by the female figure in the fresco adorning the adjacent room. Furthered by these considerations the allegory has been interpreted as an allegory of Fertility even though it does not exactly respond to the iconology sanctioned by Cesare Ripa which the other frescoes refer to[21].
The third, and last, room on the ground floor of the building is decorated with an allegoric fresco of *Sapienza* repainted in 1907 by Paolo Vetri, probably on the outlines of the preexisting 17th century composition.
The work depicts a seated woman holding an open book in her right hand and a flaming lamp in her left. At her feet is the motto «Omnia comspicuo»[22].
The series of representations of the various virtues continue in the rooms on the upper floor, which were originally destined for a public function.
The first is the vigorous finger of a bearded man wearing a crown of laurel and holding the branch of a peach tree in his right hand. The index finger of his left hand is held to his lips in the gesture of one demanding silence. The inscription at his feet reads «Eximia est virtus praestare silentia rebus».
The iconography faithfully follows the image proposed by Ripa, from whom we learn that the peach is «dedicato ad Arpocrate dio del silenzio perché ha le foglie simili alla lingua umana e il frutto rassomiglia al cuore... gli antichi vollero significare che il tacere a' suoi tempi è virtù, però l'uomo non deve consumare il tempo in molte parole vane e senza frutto, ma tacendo ha da considerare le cose prima che ne parli»[23]. One's first impulse is to interpret this image as a vague admonition to carry out the beneficial activity of loans with discretion and reserve.

B. Corenzio, *Il Silenzio*, fresco, hall of the *Monte*

Again, the *Pazienza* represented in the adjoining room — a young peasant girl carrying a yoke on her shoulders and, at her feet the inscription «Libenter» — clearly alludes to the requisite virtue in absolving the duties of the *Monte*[24]. The allegory in the third room represents *Concordia* «Una donna bella che mostri gravità, nella destra mano tenghi uno scettro che in cima habbia fiori e frutti di varie sorti, in capo ancora haverà una ghirlanda di mele granate, con le foglie e i frutti...» at her feet is «un fascio di verghe delle quali ciascuna per se stessa è debile, ma tutte insieme sono forti e dure» (Ripa)[25]. The inscription alludes to the benefits gathered by the practice of such virtue «Concordia parvae res crescunt».

The outstanding example of this virtue was provided by the *Monte* itself which, in 1539, by the modest, private initiative of two Neapolitan noblemen — Nardo di Palma and Aurelio Paparo — was transformed into a renowned banking establishment, acknowledged by the viceroy in 1584 and attaining a state of notable prosperity. In these years the sums lent amounted to 64,000 ducats and 50,000 ducats were apparently spent in the construction of the new complex[26].

Again, the two allegories, one painted in the outer sacresty and the other in the hall of the Congregation next to the chapel, tie in with the cycle. The first depicts a young woman with the terrestrial globe in one hand. She is *Eternità*, trampling on Time, represented by an old man with wings. The painting is ascribed to Paolo Vetri who probably executed it on the outlines of the pre-existing 17th century composition[27]. In the second painting, a young man with outspread wings in the act of running — perhaps alluding to the virtue of carrying out charitable works with diligence. This interpretation is confirmed by the inscription under the painting «Si bene quid facias, facies cito»[28].

Problems of Chronology

The oldest decorations, the ones from the 17th century, were all executed in slightly different time-frames. Precedence was given to the works in the main building, which was readied and made available for the first meeting of the Protectors on 7th August 1601, while the preparation of the frescoes in the various rooms was still going on in October of that year, presumably to terminate in the course of a few months[29].

The decoration of the chapel interior began in the following year although the work on the façade — including the frescoes of Rodriguez and Battistello — had been completed in the first months of 1601[30]. Also the hall of the Congregation, adjacent to the chapel, seems to have been already frescoed in October 1601. Probably work was suspended waiting for the plasterers and gilders to complete their tasks[31].

The bulk of the fresco work was, however, carried out during 1603 since we note that, on 22nd December of that year, Belisario Corenzio was paid one of the most considerable sums of the entire work — although we have evidence of request for further intervention as late as June 1604[32]. From the sound of the annotations in the «Conclusions» drawn up by the Protectors in the work journal we can deduce that delay in the execution of the frescoes in the chapel

L. RODRIGUEZ (?), *Concordia*, fresco, Building

was mainly due to Corenzio, frequently absent from work and often careless in fulfilling his obligations[33].

The oil paintings for the altar, The *Pietà*, The *Resurrezione di Cristo* and the *Assunzione della Madonna* were ordered in 1603 but only two of them were completed in that year, i.e. La *Pietà* by Fabrizio Santafede and The *Assunzione* by Ippolito Borghese. The third canvas, The *Resurrezione di Cristo* was finished at a later date owing to the death of the painter, Girolamo Imparato, who had received the initial commission. Fabrizio Santafede was assigned to complete painting[34].

With the economic recovery instigated by Carlo di Borbone in the 18th century the *Monte di Pietà* regained its former prestige and plans for important restorations were made. New projects were drawn up in the 30's and in the 40's for the complete renovation of the sacristy, with its monochrome decorations and figures, as well as for the large canvas *Carità* by Giuseppe Bonito and the wooden wardrobes lining the room.

The hall of the Congregation, with its four splendid corner cabinets, was again the object of restoration. Portraits of Carlo di Borbone and Maria Amalia di Sassonia were painted on the walls, surrounded by a myriad of floral and trompe-l'oeil architectural motifs. The vault, too, was elaborated by numerous allegorical figures and mock architectural designs around the 17th century fresco entitled *Velocità*[35].

The Decoration of the «Monte di Pietà» in the 17th Century

The frescoes in the *Monte di Pietà* were painted by the Greek artist — naturalized Neapolitan — Belisario Corenzio. According to information collected by his biographer, Bernardo De Dominici — later confirmed by newly discovered documentation — Belisario was bor~ in 1558 and some time later (at 12 years of age) moved to Naples[36]. His Greek origins are confirmed by the epitaph on his grave in the church of *SS. Severino e Sossio*. As a matter of fact, the inscription tells us that Corenzio was among the *regi stipendiari*, i.e. the Greek refugees who had from the king the special privilege of a lifetime pension[37]. The existence in Naples of the Greek family named Corenzio is documented as early as 1572. We read that this Corenzio family received a salary of 16 ducats a month[38] and more than likely Belisario was one of them[39]. His first documented work is dated 1590 and after this year the activity of Corenzio can be precisely traced; he was, in fact, commissioned for one work after another in rapid succession[40]. In 1582 Corenzio is named in a document in which a certain Giovanni di Santo Mauro stands guaranty for a sum the Greek owes to Teodato Melissena[41]. In 1594 he hired a young apprentice from Teano[42]. In 1600 his wife, Violante Morra, gave birth to their first child, Giulio Cesare. The following year their daughter, Vittoria, was born[43], and in 1608 another son, Costantino. The family lived in a house in the Montecalvario district[44].

Between 1605 and 1607 there is no documentation concerning the artist's activity in Naples so that it is presumed he was engaged at Montecassino frescoing the dome[45]. No further biographical notes are available; we only know that in 1646 he was still alive and residing at Roccaguglielma — the

F. Santafede, *Deposizione*, oil on canvas, Chapel

Another important public commission in the nineties was the *Storie della Vita di Maria* in the choir of *S. Maria La Nova*[57]. The frescoes in the vault — the first to be executed — still seem to be influenced by the early manner of Cavalier d'Arpino, while the side panels recall the Barocci aspects of d'Arpino's later, more mature work. Abandoning the abstract use of colour, the delineated chiaroscuro and gloomy tonalities, Belisario adopts a gamut of brighter and more iridescent hues[58].

At the beginning of the new century, Belisario was engaged in the fresco decoration of the *Cappella degli Angeli* in the transept of the important church of *Gesù Nuovo*. Influenced even more strongly by the followers of Barocci's school, Corenzio emphasizes the play of light and clear shadow as well as the manner of painting draperies with prismatic faceting. In the frescoes of the *Orsini* chapel in the *Gesù e Maria* church, painted in 1601, the process of adaptation to the style of Barocci - diffused in Naples by Girolamo Imparato, Teodoro d'Errico and Luigi Rodriguez — appears even more evident. The figures exult in a light and sparkling pictorial display, standing out from the background of juxtaposed points of brightness and darkness[59].

Le Storie della Passione di Cristo in the *Monte di Pietà* represent the first affirmation of the completely realized style of Corenzio. Only rarely will the artist achieve such positive results in his long and eventful career. Already in the second decade of the century Corenzio begins to show evident signs of decline, possibly due to his fear of being unable to keep in step with the evolution in the art of painting characterized by the pictorial revolution of Caravaggio and the new classicism of the Bolognese painters. Indeed, the art historian De Dominici reminds us of the deep professional jealousy displayed by Corenzio[60].

But, above all, the frescoes in the *Monte di Pietà* are important as Corenzio here realizes for the first time his «idea pittoresca, che è di ordine globale, compositivo, atmosferico» (Previtali)[61]. His painting must be interpreted as a continuum, with inseparable parts where the single figure casts off its own significance and acquires it again in relation to the other figures — like coloured blocks in a wide and uniform space, despite the forced fragmentation of the surfaces into panels and stuccoed strips.

Belisario gives free reign here to his inexhaustible narrative verve, usually adopting a type of human figure with a marked physionomy. The result is an incredibly ductile representation, lively to the point of touching comic and grotesque tones of theatricality. In these frescoes the artist reveals his familiarity with the relationship existing between painting and theatre — so important to Manneristic culture — and with the techniques essential to a blending of reality and imagination. For instance, in the *Presentazione di Cristo al Popolo* he adopts a typically Manneristic expedient to attract and involve the observer in the scenic space of the painting, portraying — among the bystanders at the extreme right — a bearded and turbaned old man who looks the observer right in the eyes, capturing his glance, imprisoning it, and inviting him to observe and react emotionally. Then again, some scenes testify to the ever-present influence of Cavalier d'Arpino despite Corenzio's convinced adhesion to the currents of Barocci, so evident in his choice of pastel tonalities and soft, iridescent technique. In the *Flagellazione di Cristo*,

B. Corenzio, *Andata al calvario*, fresco, Chapel

for example, Belisario is greatly influenced by a rather famous engraving by Cavalier d'Arpino, depicting the same scene, dated 1593 and dedicated to Cardinal Santori[62]. In the *Orazione di Cristo nell'orto* Corenzio faces new problems such as the effects of luminosity and the relation between figure and landscape, revealing his knowledge of the Venetian painters who have always considered these aspects one of their main concerns. Again, the scene of the *Cattura di Cristo*, which is customarily shown in a nocturnal light, offers the occasion to adopt a series of contrasting expedients and violent flashes of light which tend to exalt the dramatic atmosphere of the event.

It so happens that Corenzio can be considered very akin to Fabrizio Santafede, the most important exponent of the Venetian-Florentine reform of the last decade of the century in Naples[63].

In fact, the «Protectors» of the *Monte di Pietà* reserved for him the prestigious commission of the *Deposizione*, the high altar painting in the Chapel. On 19th February 1601 Santafede stipulated a contract for the painting at a price to be established, in any case not to exceed 250 ducats — receiving a down payment of 40 ducats.

On 30th July of the same year the artist was officially appointed to paint the *Deposizione* but two years later the painting had not been completed. On 22nd March and 20th May 1603 the artist received 60 ducats at a time on account[64]. The final payment of 101.80 ducats on 17th December 1603 attests to the date of conclusion of the painting[65].

The work belongs to the period of full maturity of the art of Santafede, effectually expressing the qualities typical of his painting, marked by a personal and extremely original interpretation of reformed devotional painting in Tuscany as well as Venetian pictorial art[66]. The painting on the high altar offers a contrast of severe containment and strict adherence to the religious subject with the brilliant and witty frescoes on the vaults painted by Corenzio. The dramatic moment of the deposition of the body of Christ from the cross is expressed with quiet devotion, the figures are merely lined up at the sides of the figure of Chirst, the lights — although rising from supernatural sources — seem natural, and no longer illuminate the personages in a Manneristic fashion but portray them in real life, e.g. the man depicted at the extreme right behind St. John the Evangelist[67].

Santafede was held in high esteem by the «Protectors» of the *Monte* and in a document they describe him as «homo di molto valore e che tiene nella pittura pochi pari».

They therefore decided to entrust him with the completion of the *Resurrezione*, left unfinished at the death of the painter Gerolamo Imparato. On 27th August 1607 Santafede was given the task and, in fact, completed the painting and received the final payment on 24th December 1608[68]. High in the centre of the painting Christ is depicted with the cross and the banner, rising again, and surrounded by an aureole of angels. An uncovered sarcophagus stands in the lower part of the painting, surrounded by still-sleeping soldiers and others who, on awakening, stare in dismay at the miracle. According to old Neapolitan guidebooks, one of the sleeping soldiers in the foreground is a self-portrait of the artist[69]. The work is signed on one side of the sarchophagus with the painter's intertwined initials.

B. Corenzio, *Incoronazione di spine*, fresco, Chapel

B. Corenzio, *Ecce Homo*, fresco, Chapel

B. CORENZIO, *Cristo davanti a Pilato*, fresco, Chapel

B. Corenzio, *Cristo nell'orto*, fresco, Chapel

B. Corenzio, *Cattura di Cristo*, fresco, Chapel

B. CORENZIO, *Cristo nel limbo*, fresco, Chapel

B. Corenzio, *Angelo*, fresco, Chapel

B. Corenzio, *Angelo reggitenda*, fresco, Chapel

F. Santafede (signed), *Resurrezione di Cristo*, oil on canvas, Chapel

The first work on the canvas attributable to Imparato can be discerned from the more fragmentary character of the composition of the scene and «dal permanere di una interpretazione ad effetti di vago luminismo, oltre che nelle figure della zona superiore, di quelle forme sfatte ed ombrate, che l'Imparato assumeva dai riflessi del manierismo senese»[70]. However, the work shows the preference given by Santafede to a nocturnal illumination offering the possibility of refracting the light on the crest of the draperies according to the manner reflecting Venetian inspiration[71].

The third large painting on the left altar of the chapel, the *Assunzione della Vergine* is by Ippolito Borghese, the Umbrian painter from Sigillo, a little village near Gubbio. The work is signed by the artist on a torn bit of paper lying on the floor in the lower right of the canvas[72]. Around the empty sepulchre of the Madonna the twelve apostles stand in wonderment or in contemplation; on high some youthful angels carry the kneeling Madonna to heaven on a cloud; at the sides a chorus of angels play musical instruments and a group of winged cherubs form a crown around the holy figure; in the centre of the painting the distant background reveals a scene with Renaissance architecture.

On 13th February 1603 the «Protectors» of the *Monte* commissioned Borghese to paint the *Assunzione* together with another canvas, the *Resurrezione*, which later, with Borghese's assent, passed to Imparato on 20th March of that same year and, as we have seen, was completed by Fabrizio Santafede.

The *Assunzione della Vergine*, together with other notable paintings, is among the first works of the artist in Naples. Borghese's style is reminiscent of his study of the Sienese painters influenced by Barocci, particularly Francesco Vanni, and by his knowledge of the sacred paintings of Cavalier d'Arpino and the Tuscan reformed painters[73]. According to De Dominici, Borghese apparently painted a *Pietà* for the *Monte* as well, recognized today as the signed canvas hanging in the *Pinacoteca Provinciale* at Bari, on loan from the *Museo di Capodimonte*, Naples.

The *Pietà* was probably done in the same years as the *Assunzione*, the two works representing one of the most fruitful moments in the artistic career of the painter. The intermingling of Barocci-Sienese accents with «un cromatismo più venetizzante caratteristico di alcuni pittori fiorentini come, per esempio, Cigoli» is indeed original[74]. A Tuscan influence is also evident in the «panneggiare ampio e morbido delle vesti» of the Apostles[75].

The Decoration of the Halls in the «Monte di Pietà»

Documents bearing the dates of 19th, 20th and 26th February 1601[76] testify that Luigi Rodriguez and Battistello Caracciolo were active in the *Monte* along with Belisario. On 19th February 1601 the «Protectors» paid 12 ducats to Rodriguez for the fresco figures of *Fede* and *Speranza* as well as four little angels on the façade; Battistello Caracciolo received 6 ducats for the six cherubs in the three panels crowning the façade. On 20th and 26th February they received the same sum, separately, a second time. Only faint traces of Rodriguez's work remain, fragmentary shadows revealing only that the figures were represented in a mock architectural space crowned by a pair of little angels. The Battistello angels are practically invisible from below, as well, but fortunately the artist used the technique of incising the outlines of the figures onto the plaster and today they are visible at close quarters. Two angels are seen in each panel and in the central one they stand at the sides of the marble crest of the *Monte* holding a long inscription in their hands reading «O Magnum Pietatis Opus». These figures assume particular importance since they constitute the first documented work by Caracciolo. They reveal a conception which still leans towards Mannerism and are similar, for example, to the «putti» holding back the draperies painted by Belisario on the counterfaçade and to the ones entwined in flight in the fresco of *Agricoltura* in the Hall of the *Monte*. However, these plump, smiling faces, with their soft look, can easily be distinguished from the «putti» by Corenzio thanks to their heightened vivacity and freshness of expression. The minute strokes etched along the roundish outline of the cheeks and chin recall the sparing and precise techniqe — like an engraving — of the early drawings by Battistello[77]. The presence of Rodriguez and Battistello can also be perceived in some frescoes in the Halls of the *Monte*, paid to Belisario and attributed to him in the old Neapolitan guidebooks[78].

The allegory of *Fecondità* frescoed in one of the rooms on the ground floor reveals — in comparison with the *Agricoltura* in the adjacent room — a more monumental conception of the human figure. Beneath the draperies the observer can perceive the well-turned volume of the body, the legs resolutely planted on the earth. The light is firmly oriented from left to right and the shadows thicken on the side of the figure unexposed to the luminous glow because of the slight inclination of the upper part of the body. In my opinion we are dealing with a personality quite different from Belisario. Here is a painter who looks more to the reformed Tuscans, and perhaps to Ciampelli in particular, than to Cavalier d'Arpino, and who tends to leave behind the late-Manneristic inheritance in order to reach a more personal vision characterized by a retrieval of the grandeur and monumentality of the human figure. In comparison, the figure of *Agricoltura* appears more awkward, the dimensions more thickset, the source of light more vaguely orientated. The expression of the face, saddened by the thickening shadows gathering in the eyes — so typical of Belisario — still tends to be over-emphasized.

The expression of the face of the *Fecondità* is decidedly more real — the mere hint of a smile, the slightly dreamy eyes are similar to those of the angels on the façade. Even while realizing the difficulty of proposing attributions to Battistello owing to the lack of comparable works of the same period, the writer would assign this fresco to the painter in a phase of his work close upon the period of the little angels on the façade, i.e. 1601. Two pairs of angels are represented in the upper and lower areas of the fresco; one couple flanks the crest of the *Monte* while the other carries an inscription relating to the allegorical figure. In the first duo of angels one is struck by the vivacity and mobility of the faces, the floating airiness of their wings and their hair, so similar to the work of Rodriguez; in the second pair there is marked affinity with the type of angel painted by Francesco Curia[79].

As for the *Concordia*, on the first floor of the *Monte*, we would put forth the attribution to Luigi Rodriguez, the Sicilian painter documented in Naples

B. Caracciolo, *Façade*, Chapel

Sacristy

G. Bonito, *Virtù*, fresco, Sacristy

from 1594 to 1606, author of the majestic *Trinità e Santi* in the *Capodimonte Museum*[80]. The figure of the *Concordia* abounds with characteristics similar to the ones appearing in the works of Rodriguez — the elegant carriage, the slender proportion of the figures, the light and airy drapery, the colour laid on in subtle, superposed veils and, in the angels, that smiling air of quiet joy that could almost be defined as neo-Correggio, seen also in the panels in *Capodimonte*.

XVIII Century Repairs of the Chapel

Carlo di Borbone had only recently been entroned in Naples when the «Protectors» of the *Monte* set up a program for the restoration of the rooms adjacent to the chapel, for the sacristy and the Hall of the Congregation. Documents from 1763 refer to the works of gilding the walls of the sacristy. The same date is given to the four monochrome frescoes representing *Virtù*, by Giuseppe Bonito (reported verbally by Nicola Spinosa) and the entire decoration of the walls with vegetable motifs[81].

The large ceiling canvas depicting *Carità* is also by the hand of Bonito, dated 1742 (at the lower left, next to the signature). Giuseppe Bonito is truly the dominant artist in this extremely refined sacristy, having also painted the two small pictures on copper representing *L'Orazione nell'Orto* and *La Pietà* seen on the genuflectories flanking the walnut-root wardrobe of the same period. This piece is decorated with gilded bronze ornaments in a floral motif, volutes and small consoles; the top frieze — with the *Monte* crest at the centre — is done in decorative motifs in carved and gilded wood. The wardrobe has been ascribed to Giovanni Sisto, furniture maker and author of the shelves in the Archives of the *Palazzo Loreto* at Mercogliano[82]. Recent documentary evidence reveals that the small paintings on copper were done in 1744 (the artist was paid for them on 23rd December 1744)[83], the same stylistic period of the *Carità* on the ceiling. Bonito had reached a full maturity of expression in the works created in the fourth decade of the XVIII century, handing down to posterity the most significant results of his career. References to the pictorial production of the mature Solimena are evident in these works and it is through him that Bonito goes back to the 17th century sources delineated in the paintings of Mattia Preti and Luca Giordano. For example, in the *Carità*, the prospective glimpses and the accentuated scenographic effect of the background architecture recall the examples of Mattia Preti in his canvases at *S. Pietro a Maiella*[84]. The paintings on copper reveal a research for chromatic preciousness in the glazed and brilliant colours typical of that technique[85]. Renovation of the opposite side of the building was begun in the same years, in the *Sala delle Cantoniere* or *Sala della Congregazione*. The four allegories of the «*Seasons*» were painted on mock architectural panels. The sole testimony of the more antique decoration, the figure of *Velocità*, was preserved, but was almost entirely repainted during the restoration at the beginning of this century[86]. For the walls, the Protectors of the *Monte* commissioned the portraits of Carlo di Borbone and Maria Amalia di Sassonia within a trompe-l'oeil frame bordered by military trophies. Four «cantoniere» or corner pieces, were placed at each corner of the room — identical, with two

Sacristy, Interior.

G. Bonito, *Carità*, oil on canvas, Sacristy

«Sala delle Cantoniere».
Neapolitan artists (middle of XVIII century), detail of the corner pieces.

Neapolitan artists (middle of XVIII century), detail of the corner pieces

B. Caracciolo (?), *Fecondità*, fresco

B. CORENZIO, *Agricoltura*, fresco, Building

B. CARACCIOLO (?), Detail of «stemma» (coat of arms) - bearing angels

orders, decorated and bombé. These corner cupboards reflect the decorative, pictorial taste seen on the walls. A soft green background displays lacquered flowers, stylized vegetable motifs and volutes while, in the centre of the two orders, moulded and gilded frames encompass two ovals depicting mythological divinities carried on carts. These painted scenes are the work of a fairly good Neapolitan painter, follower of Francesco de Mura, whereas the carvings show an affinity with others executed towards the middle of the century — for example, with the carvings on the wardrobes in the *Farmacia degli Incurabili*. The motif of the tiny head visible on the frame of the second order is seen again in the frames on the four allegories of the *Pietà* executed by Francesco de Mura for the *Monte* in 1759. The possibility exists, therefore, that the same craftsman did the frames of these paintings as well as the ones on the corner pieces in the *Sala delle Cantoniere*[87].

As for the decor of the ceiling, the manner of the painter is bound to the Neapolitan scenographic tradition of the beginning of the century, identified in Vincenzo Re and Cristoforo Russo — as kindly reported to me by Rosanna Cioffi.

In particular, this scholar recognizes the hand of Francesco Russo, son of Cristoforo, author of the pictorial decorations on the ceiling of the chapel of *Raimondo di Sangro, Principe di San Severo*[88].

The same painter can also be distinguished in the portraits of Carlo and Maria Amalia on the walls, where the trompe-l'oeil motifs of the frame resemble the ones that appear on the tomb of Raimondo di Sangro, designed by Russo[89].

[1] Cnf. DE DOMINICI, *Vite de' pittori scultori e architetti napoletani*, Napoli, 1742, vol. II, p. 305, for what concerns the biography pp. 292-318.

[2] As regards B. De Dominici cnf F. BOLOGNA, *Francesco Solimena, Napoli, 1958, pp. 157-161;* G. PREVITALI, *La fortuna dei primitivi dal Vasari ai neoclassici*, Torino, 1964, pp. 67-68; F. BOLOGNA, *I pittori alla corte angioina di Napoli*, Roma, 1969, pp. 4-7, idem, *La coscienza dell'arte d'Italia*, Torino, 1982, pp. 128, 142-143.

[3] See the report by De Dominici about Belisario's bad behaviour towards Annibale Carracci (surely invented as Annibale never came to Naples), Guido Reni and his apprentice Francesco Gessi, Cavalier D'Arpino and Domenichino and finally on the poisoning of Luigi Rodriguez, his apprentice, cnf. B. DE DOMINICI, *op. cit.*, pp. 296 and foll.

[4] Idem, op. cit., p. 296 and 302; De Dominici (p. 316) quotes a brief biography of Corenzio by Paolo De Matteis (according to him) underlying the positive judgement here contained. The Neapolitan historian reports also that Francesco Solimena referred to De Matteis as «il Belisario dè tempi nostri». Maybe the first hint to the consideration of De Dominici about Corenzio as «pre-baroque» was given him by Solimena himself who was his master. The Neapolitan historian refers also to a biography by Massimo Stanzione in which the author is said to have defined Corenzio as «pieno di Gran Invenzione, non scelto». This biography is in a manuscript (may-be by De Dominici himself) kept at the National Library of Naples, cnf. F. FARAGLIA, «Le memorie degli artisti napoletani pubblicate dal De Dominici», in *Archivio Storico per le provincie napoletane 1883*, 8, pp. 82-117 and especially 107. Nothing of particular interest, compared to De Dominici, is contained in the biography of Corenzio by O. GIANNONE, *Giunte sulle vite dè pittori napoletani*, Napoli, 1773, reccommended edition edited by O. Morisani, Napoli, 1941, pp. 95-98.

[5] B. DE DOMINICI, *Vite dè pittori... cit.*, p. 315.

[6] Cnf. L. LANZI, *Storia pittorica d'Italia*, Bassano, 1795-96, recommended edition Firenze, 1845, pp. 267-268.

[7] Cnf. The following paragraph.

[8] Cnf. C. D'ENGENIO, *Napoli Sacra*, Napoli, 1624, pp. 334-336, P. SARNELLI, *Guida dè forestieri*, Napoli, 1686, p. 212, G.C. CAPACCIO, *Il Forestiero. Dialoghi in X Giornate*, Napoli, 1634, p. 917-918.

[9] Cnf. G. SIGISMONDO, *Descrizione della città di Napoli e suoi borghi*, Napoli, 1788, pp. 88-90.

[10] Cnf. C. CELANO - G. CHIARINI, *Notizie del Bello, dell'Antico e del Curioso della città di Napoli*, Napoli, 1856, III, pp. 749-51.

[11] Cnf. F. COLONNA STIGLIANO, «La Cappella di Sansevero e D. Raimondo Di Sangro. I. Introduzione» in: *Napoli nobilissima*, 1984, IV, p. 34; Idem, «La Cappella di Sansevero e D. Raimondo Di Sangro III Raimondo Di Sangro: La sua vita e le sue invenzioni», Idem, p. 93; G. CECI, «IL PALAZZO DI GRAVINA III» IN *Napoli Nobilissima*, 1897, VI, p. 31.

[12] Cnf. B. DE DOMINICI, *op. cit.*, pp. 293, 298, 313 foll.

[13] Cnf. N. FARAGLIA, «Memorie artistiche della chiesa benedettina dè SS. Severino e Sossio di Napoli», in *Archivio Storico per le Province Napoletane*, 1878, 3, pp. 243-248; IDEM, «Notizie di alcuni artisti che lavorarono nella chiesa di S. Martino e nel Tesoro di San Gennaro», *ibidem* 1885, X, pp. 441-442; IDEM, «La Sala del catasto onciario nell'archivio di stato» II, in *Napoli Nobilissima* 1899, VII, pp. 86-87; G. CECI, «S. Marcellino» II, in *Napoli nobilissima* 1895, VI, p. 123; IDEM, «La chiesa e la festa di Piedigrotta» II, in *Napoli Nobilissima* 1895, IV, p. 116; A. COLOMBO, «Il Monastero e la Chiesa di S. Maria della Sapienza», in *Napoli Nobilissima* 1902, XI, pp. 62-68; IDEM «S. Andrea delle Dame I, il Monastero» in *Napoli Nobilissima* 1904, XIII, pp. 51-52 and pp. 108-109; G. D'ADDOSIO, «Illustrazioni e documenti sulla cripta di S. Andrea di Amalfi e S. Matteo di Salerno» in *Archivio Storico per le province napoletane*, 1909, 34, pp. 28-foll.; IDEM, «Documenti inediti di artisti napoletani dei secoli XVI e XVII dalle Polizze dei Banchi»; ibidem, 1919, 44, pp. 385-387.

[14] W. ROLFS, *Geschichte der Malerei Neapels*, Leipzig, 1910, pp. 216-222; G. SOBOTKA, item «Corenzio Belisario», in U. THIEME - F. BECKER, *Allgemeines Lerikon der Bildenden Kunstler*, Leipzig, 1912, VII, pp. 409-412.

[15] Among the first studies the catalogue of the art exhibition edited by F. BOLOGNA - R. CAUSA, *Fontainbleau e la Maniera Italiana*, Napoli, 1952, and the volume F. BOLOGNA, *Roviale Spagnolo e la pittura napoletana del Cinquecento*, Napoli, 1959.

[16] Cnf. G. PREVITALI, «La pittura napoletana dalla venuta di Teodoro d'Errico (1574) a quella di Michelangelo da Caravaggio (1607)» in *Storia di Napoli*, Cava dei Tirreni, 1972, pp. 880-882; IDEM, *La pittura del Cinquecento a Napoli e nel Vicereame*, Torino, 1978, pp. 117-119.

[17] W. VITZTHUM, «Neapolitan Seicento Drawings in Florida», in *The Burlington Magazine*, 1961, CIII, p. 313; C. MONBEIG-GOGUEL, W. VITZTHUM, *Le dessin à Naples du XVI siècle au XVIII siècle*, catalogue of the art exhibition, Paris, 1967, pp. 5-8; W. VITZTHUM-A.M. PETRIOLI, *Cento disegni napoletani dei secoli XVI-XVIII*, catalogue of the art-exhibition, Firenze, 1967; W. VITZTHUM, *Disegni napoletani del Sei e del Settecento*, catalogue of the art-exhibition, Roma, 1969-70, pp. 9-10.

[18] For the meaning of the subjects of the marble decoration on the front cnf. the essay by MARIA IDA CATALANO in this volume: *Plastic Decoration*. The decoration of the façade was completed by the two figures of *Fede* and *Speranza* frescoed by Luigi Rodriguez in February, 1601 at the two sides of the window on the second order of the front. They were placed in a mock architectonic niche and were surmounted by a pair of little angels. Unfortunately, they are today scarcely visible because of their bad conditions. The rain and other atmospherical elements have spoiled their pictorial pigment. The six little angels painted contemporarily by Battistello Caracciolo in the four panels decorating the façade are also hardly discernible. Thanks to the contours engraved on the plaster, still visible at the two sides of the marble symbol of the *Monte*, it is possible to perceive two little angels who hold an inscription *O Magnum Pietatis Opus*. The same inscription may be found on the marble fascia of the trabeation. For what concerns the documents of payment to Luigi Rodriguez and Battistello Caracciolo for the frescoes of the façade and to Alessandro Hernandez for the frames, cnf. M. MORELLI - L. CONFORTI, *La Cappella del Monte di Pietà*, Napoli, 1899, p. 39 and the documentary appendix by E. Nappi in this volume.

[19] «A 19 d'agosto 1602. Che si dia a Bellisario la lista de li' Misteri della Passione p. la Cappella», cnf. M. MORELLI - L. CONFORTI, op. cit., p. 26 and the documentary appendix by E. Nappi in this volume.

[20] For what concerns the figure of agriculture, cnf. C. RIPA, *Iconologia di Cesare Ripa Perugino cavaliere dei Santi Maurizio e Lazaro divisa in tre libri nei quali si esprimono varie immagini di Virtù, Vitij, Passioni umane, Affetti, Atti, Discipline, Humori, Elementi, Corpi Celesti, Provincie d'Italia, Fiumi e altre materie infinite utili ad ogni Stato di Persone. Ampliata dal sig. cav. Gio. Zaratino Castellini Romano Venetia 1645*. Book I, p. 15. Agriculture is thus described by Ripa: «Donna vestita di verde con una ghirlanda di spighe di grano in capo, nella sinistra mano tenga il circolo dei dodici segni celesti abbracciando con la destra un arbuscello che fiorisca mirandolo, fisso ai piedi vi farà un aratro. Il vestimento verde significa la Speranza senza la quale non sarebbe chi si desse giammai la fatica di lavorare e coltivare la terra. La corona di spighe si dipinge per lo principal fine di quest'arte che è di far moltiplicar le biade, che son necessarie a mantener la vita dell'huomo. L'abbracciar l'arbuscello fiorito e il riguardarlo fisso significa l'amore dell'agricoltura verso le piante che sono quasi sue figlie attendendone il desiato frutto, che nel fiorire gli promettono. I dodici segni sono i vari tempi dell'anno e le stagioni che da essa Agricoltura si considerano. L'Aratro si dipinge come istrumento principalissimo di quest'arte». As you can see, this description of the fresco completely corresponds to the description made by Ripa except for the plough which is not mentioned here and the different position of the attributes, the globe in her right hand and the flowering branch in her left.

[21] I have not been able to find this description in Ripa; the dish full of fruit that the woman offers and the inscription supported by the two little angels *Fructum Offert* seem to allude to fertility, even if the cornucopia — that is not represented here — is the main attribute to fertility. The dolphin painted at the woman's feet is the symbol of salvation, cnf. C. RIPA, op. cit., Book, III, p. 543. B. MOLAJOLI, in *Opere d'arte nel Banco di Napoli*, Napoli, 1953, p. 42, was the first to identify this figure with Fertility. He also identifies the previous figure with the Earth. B. MOLAJOLI, op. cit., p. 42.

[22] Cnf. the description in C. RIPA, op. cit., Book III, p. 545: «Sapienza. Giovane in notte vestita di colore turchino nella destra mano tiene una lampada piena d'olio acceso e nella sinistra un libro. Si dipinge giovane perché ha dominio sopra le stelle che non l'invecchiano né le tolgono l'intelligenza de' secreti di Dio, i quali sono vivi e veri eternamente. La lampada accesa è il lume dell'intelletto il quale per particolar dono di Dio arde nell'anima nostra senza mai consumarsi o sminuirsi, solo avviene per nostro particolare mancamento che venga spesso in gran parte offuscato, e ricoperto da vitij che sono le tenebre le quali soprabbondano nell'anima e occupando la Vita del lume fanno estinguere la Sapienza, e introducono in suo luogo l'ignoranza e i cattivi pensieri... Il libro si pone per la Bibbia che vuol dire libro dei libri perché in esso si impara tutta la Sapienza che è necessaria per farli salvi».

[23] Cnf. C. RIPA, op. cit., Book III, p. 570.

[24] Cnf. C. RIPA, op. cit., Book II, pp. 474-475: «Donna vestita di berrettino accompagnato col taneto, con un giogo in spalla in sembiante modesto e umile. La Pazienza consiste in tollerare fortemente le cose avverse, è uno dei principali effetti della fortezza la quale si stende fino al soffrire il giogo della servitù, con l'animo intrepido e costante, quando la necessità lo richiede. Il vestimento del color suddetto significa Pazienza per avvicinarsi molto al nero... Il giogo è significativo della Pazienza la quale come si è detto si esercita solo nel tollerare le avversità con animo costante e tranquillo....

[25] Cnf. C. RIPA, op. cit., Book I, p. 97 where the phrase is quoted *Concordia parvae res crescunt*.

[26] Cnf. R. FILANGIERI, *I banchi di Napoli dalle origini alla costituzione del Banco delle due Sicilie (1539-1808)*, Napoli, 1940, vol. 1, pp. 31-45; Idem, *I Banchi di Napoli*. Continuation of fasc. VI for the IV centennial anniversary of the foundation of the «Banco di Napoli», Napoli, 1941, pp. 11-12.

[27] Cnf. C. RIPA, op. cit., Book I, p. 163. According to Ripa this is the iconography of the medals of the empire period particularly of the empress Faustina: «donna in piedi, in habito di matrona e in capo un velo che li cuopra le spalle. Lo star in piedi senza alcuna dimostrazione di movimento ci fa comprendere che nell'Eternità non vi è moto, né mutazione nel tempo o delle cose naturali o delle intelleggibili... La ragione perché questa figura non si faccia à sedere essendo il sedere inditio di maggior stabilità, e che il sedere si suol notare quasi sempre nella quiete, che è correlativa del moto e senza il quale non si può esso intendere e non essendo compresa sotto questo genere la quiete dell'Eternità ne anche si deve esprimere in questa maniera, ancorché da tutti non sia affermato, come si dirà qui di sotto. Si fa donna per la conformità del nome, Matrona d'età stabile. Tiene il mondo in mano perché il mondo produce il tempo, con la sua mobilità e significa che l'Eternità è fuori del mondo. Il velo, che ambedue gli omeri le copre, mostra che quel tempo, che non è presente nell'Eternità, s'occulta,

essendovi eminentemente». Time is represented as «Homo vecchio alato... che mostrerà di andare con la tardità e lentezza... Si fà alato secondo il detto *Volat irreparabilis tempis* il che è tanto chiaro per esperienza, che per non disacerbare le piaghe della nostra miseria, non occorre farvi lungo discorso». Cnf. C. RIPA, *Iconologia...* cit., Book III, p. 620.

[28] It does not seem possible to identify this figure as Molajoli does, with *Soccorso* because the iconography of Succour is generally different from this representation. Cnf. C. RIPA..., op. cit., Book III, p. 580. For what concerns *Velocità*, too, the XVI century iconography scholar gives us a slightly different description: «Donna con l'ali alle spalle in atto di correre tenga uno sparviero in capo con l'ali aperte...» or «Donna con l'ali alle spalle portando i talari, ovvero stivaletti simili a quelli di Mercurio e nella destra mano una saetta...», Idem, p. 645.

[29] R. FILANGIERI, op. cit., p. 44.

[30] Cnf. M. MORELLI - L. CONFORTI, op. cit., p. 39. documents taken from the Historical Archive of the Banco di Napoli in *Rassegna Economica* IX (1939) p. 480; see also the documentary appendix by E. Nappi in this volume.

[31] For the fresco of *Velocità* cnf. M. MORELLI - L. CONFORTI, op. cit., p. 25 and B. Molajoli, op. cit., p. 43; for the payment to the stucco workers and to the gilders of 31 May 1603 cnf. M. MORELLI - L. CONFORTI, op. cit., p. 26.

[32] On 22 December 1603, Corenzio received the last 420 ducats of the 600 paid to him for the paintings «della Cappella e fuori di quella e sopra la porta del Monte et al muro dove si impegna i pegni»; cnf. the document found by E. Nappi and published in the documentary appendix to this volume. Evidently, Corenzio frescoed the wall of the counter-façade and «il muro dove si impegna nel cortile». This last is no more recognizable because the frescoes are not visible any more. Cnf. the document of 4 june 1604 in the documentary appendix.

[33] In particular cnf. two documents of 1603, the first of 27 February in which it is asked to Mario Capece Bozzuto to call for Belisario so that he «possa ordinarli che finischi quanto prima la pittura della Cappella», the second of 20 March in which the «Protectors» complained about Belisario «perché non cura di venire ad attendere di finire la pittura della nostra Cappella» even if he had already received the 100 ducats. Both in M. MORELLI - L. CONFORTI, *La cappella...*, op. cit., p. 25.

[34] Cnf. F. FERRANTE, *Il patrimonio artistico del Banco di Napoli*, Napoli, 1984, p. 30, together with the preceeding bibliography. Cnf. also the documentary appendix by E. Nappi in this volume.

[35] Cnf. B. MOLAJOLI, op. cit., pp. 41-43, cnf. also R. RUOTOLO, in *Il patrimonio artistico...*, op. cit., p. 116 and L. GIUSTI, in *Il patrimonio artistico...*, op. cit., p. 120. Cnf. also the documents of 7 July 1736 found by E. Nappi. In these documents we may found some news about some gilding-works may-be preparatory to Bonito's intervention.

[36] Cnf. B. DE DOMINICI, op. cit., p. 292 and the recently published D. AMBRASI, «Dati biografici del pittore Belisario Corenzio» in *Archivio Storico per le Province Napoletane*, 1963, pp. 383-389.

[37] Cnf. D. AMBRASI, op. cit., pp. 387-389.

[38] Cnf. the document published in N. FARAGLIA, *La sala del Catasto...*, op. cit., 1899, pp. 86-87. In the document *Estamati Corenzi* and *Gioan Corenzi suo figlio* with *loro famiglie* are named.

[39] Perhaps his father Giovanni is that Giovanni (Estamati Corenzi's son) who appears in the document of 1572.

[40] Cnf. G. D'ADDOSIO, *Documenti inediti ...*, op. cit., 1913, pp. 48-53.

[41] Cnf. G. FILANGIERI, *Documenti per la storia, le arti e le industrie delle provincie napoletane*, Napoli, 1891, vol. V, pp. 140-141.

[42] Ibidem, p. 140.

[43] Cnf. L. SALAZAR, «La fede di morte dello Spagnoletto ed altri documenti inediti intorno ad artisti napoletani del secolo XVII», in *Napoli Nobilissima*, 1896, V, p. 31.

[44] Cnf. G. D'ADDOSIO, *Documenti inediti...*, op. cit., 1913, p. 51 and p. 53.

[45] Cnf. A. CARAVITA, *I codici e le arti a Montecassino*, Montecassino, 1869-70, vol. III, p. 214.

[46] Cnf. D. AMBRASI, cit., p. 383-389. The news reported by De Dominici about Corenzio's death is not well-founded. According to the scholar, Corenzio died in 1643, falling from a scaffolding in the church of *SS. Severino e Sossio* where he was retouching some characters he had previously painted. Cnf. B. DE DOMINICI, op. cit., p. 314.

[47] Cnf. the unpublished documents and the well-founded arguing of W. PROHASKA in «Beiträge zu Giovanni Battista Caracciolo», in *Jarbuch der Kunsthistorischen Sammlungen in Wein*, 74, 1978, pp. 224-225.

[48] Not only Belisario carefully follows Cavalier D'Arpino's style but he also takes some of his characters from his paintings as the bearded man sitting at the extreme right of the fresco *Martirio*. It recalls the group on the right of Cavalier D'Arpino's *Canonizzazione di San Francesco di Paola* in the cloister of *Trinità dei Monti* in Rome. For the Roman fresco and the preliminary drawing of the group kept in the *Gabinetto disegni e stampe degli Uffizi* cnf. H. ROETTGEN, *Il Cavalier D'Arpino*, catalogue of the art-exhibition, Roma, 1973, pp. 22-23 e p. 146.

[49] Cnf. R. CAUSA, *L'arte nella Certosa di San Martino*, Napoli, 1973, pp. 32-33; H. Roettgen, op. cit., pp. 27-28, G. PREVITALI, *La pittura del Cinquecento...*, op. cit., pp. 115-116.

[50] Cnf. R. CAUSA, op. cit., pp. 50-51.

[51] Giovanni Previtali rightly mantains that De Dominici's theory about Corenzio's education is not well- founded. As a matter of fact, having found some common features between Corenzio and Tintoretto, such as that of being great fresco-workers, De Dominici mantains that Corenzio's education comes from Venetian and particularly Tintoretto painting; cnf. G. PREVITALI, *La pittura del cinquecento...*, op. cit., 1978, p. 118.

[52] Cnf. G. PREVITALI, *La pittura del Cinquecento...*, op. cit., pp. 99 and 150, n. 82.

[53] See for instance the panel with the *Nascita di Maria* by Belisario, similar to that of Marco Pino with the same subject in the church of *SS. Severino e Sossio*.

[54] But in the frescoes is already possible to catch the strong narrative *verve* and a tendency to the strong typologies that distinguishes Corenzio's painting from that of Cavalier D'Arpino which is more pondered and almost Manneristic.

[55] Cnf. A. COLOMBO, op. cit. pp. 51-52 and 108-109, G. D'ADDOSIO, *Documenti...*, op. cit., p. 49; the scenes of the presbytery were concluded in 1596 cnf. A. COLOMBO, op. cit., p. 109.

[56] Corenzio seems to have been deeply influenced by Hendrick Goltzius' prints as for the upside-down foreshortened angel of the *Martirio di S. Lucia* which derives from the print of 1587 the *Matrimonio di Cupido e Psiche*, based on a drawing by Bartolomeo Spranger. For what concerns the landscape with the sunrise in the same painting, the artist was inspired by the landscape of the print *Vista*, of the series *Cinque Sensi* made and published by Goltzius for Philippe Galle. In the female bodies too, drawned with long limbs and small heads it is possible to see the strong influence of international Mannerism and particularly of Bartolomeo Spranger. For what concerns international Mannerism influence on Corenzio, cnf. G. PREVITALI, *La pittura del Cinquecento...*, op. cit., p. 118.

[57] They can be dated starting from 1600, cnf. G. ROCCO, *Il convento e la chiesa di S. Maria La Nova*, Napoli, 1940, pp. 51 and 59. Cnf. also G. D'ADDOSIO, «Documenti inediti» in *Archivio Storico per le Provincie Napoletane*, 1917, 42, pp. 119-120.

[58] We have to mention the presence in these years of the Sicilian painter influenced by Barocci, Luigi Rodriguez in *S. Maria La Nova*. Belisario seems to have had some relations with him even before their collaboration in the *Monte di Pietà*. For what concerns the *Visione di Santa Elisabetta d'Ungheria* by Rodriguez in *S. Maria La Nova*, cnf. F. STRAZZULLO, *Postille alla «Guida Sacra della città di Napoli» del Galante*, Napoli, 1962, p. 25; for the portrait of this important artist see G. PREVITALI, *La pittura del cinquecento*, op. cit., 1978, p. 116 and p. 145, n. 73.

[59] Owing to the bad conditions of the XVIII century repaintings, the frescoes of the chapel of the treasure of *SS. Annunziata* are not well visible. They were executed in 1598-99 with the collaboration of Avanzino Nucci, one of the painters of the Sistina equipe of the Scala Santa, engaged in the *Certosa di San Martino*; cnf. G. D'ADDOSIO, *Documenti inediti...*, op. cit., pp. 49-50. Before that time, in 1595, Corenzio and Avanzino Nucci had worked together in the church of *S. Maria di Costantinopoli*; cnf. G. D'ADDOSIO, *Documenti inediti...* op. cit., p. 182. As for the frescoes of the Orsini Chapel in the church of *Gesù e Maria* cnf. DON FASTIDIO, «La cappella degli Orsini nella Chiesa del Gesù e Maria», in *Napoli Nobilissima*, 1903, XII, pp. 30-31.

[60] Cnf. B. DE DOMINICI, op. cit., pp. 292 and foll.

[61] Cnf. G. PREVITALI, *La pittura del Cinquecento...*, op. cit., pp. 118-119. Among numerous critical hints that can be found in this book, it is particularly interesting the observation about the role Corenzio's work will have in Naples about a century later. In fact, it will be an example for baroque painters and particularly for Luca Giordano. This event is indirectly confirmed — as Previtali noted — by the mistakes of attribution Corenzio-Giordano made by those who studied the drawings which were mentioned in W. VITZTHUM, *Cento disegni...*, op. cit., 1967, p. 15. A partial critical acknowledgement of the influence of Corenzio on Neapolitan baroque painters was already in the biography of the Greek painter by Bernardo De Dominici in his «Vite»; cnf. B. DE DOMINICI, op. cit., p. 315 and *Criticism about Corenzio* in this volume.

[62] For what concerns the engraving *Flagellazione* by Cavalier D'Arpino cnf. H. ROETTGEN, op. cit., pp. 174-175. Compared with this the *Flagellazione* of the *Monte di Pietà* shows some changes, as the position of the flagellants. Also some small changes in their gestures have been introduced and the point of view is lower while the painted architectures are wider. Corenzio's painting and the popular theatre have been connected by G. PREVITALI, *La pittura del cinquecento...*, op. cit., pp. 118-119. For what concerns the relationship between fiction and reality in Manneristic painting cnf A. PINELLI, *La maniera: definizione di campo e modelli di lettura*, Torino, 1981, pp. 150-166.

[63] Among Corenzio's paintings connected with Venetian and Bassano's works see most of all the *Adorazione dei pastori e committente* made on copper and kept in the Museum of *Capodimonte*, that has been possibly made by the artist more or less in the same period of the frescoes of the *Monte di Pietà* as Previtali mantains in G. PREVITALI, *La pittura del cinquecento...*, op. cit., 1978, p. 150, n. 82.

[64] For the painting of the *Pietà* by Fabrizio Santafede cnf. F. FERRANTE, in *Il patrimonio artistico del Banco di Napoli*, Napoli, 1984, pp. 26-28 together with the preceeding bibliography; for the documents of 9 February, 30 July 1601 and 20 May 1603 cnf. G. FILANGIERI, op. cit. VI, pp. 419 and 44 and M. MORELLI - L. CONFORTI, op. cit. pp. 33-34. For the document of 22 March 1603 cnf. E. NAPPI in the documentary appendix.

[65] Cnf. the document found by NAPPI in the documentary appendix of this volume.

[66] For what concerns the figure of Santafede cnf. G. PREVITALI, *La pittura del Cinquecento...* op. cit. 1978, pp. 120-122.

[67] Cnf. F. FERRANTE, op. cit., p. 28.

[68] Cnf. the complete text of the document of 27 August 1607 in which the «protettori» express very favourable opinions about Santafede (in the documentary appendix by E. NAPPI). In the appendix see also the document of final payment of 24 December. On that occasion Fabrizio Santafede promised to give to the «protettori» of the *Monte* a painting of *Cristo Flagellato* to be put in the room of hearings of the *Banco*. Probably the painting has to be identified with the *Ecce Homo* of the *Galleria del Banco di Napoli* attributed by Molajoli to an unknown Manneristic Venetian painter of the middle of XVI

century. On the contrary, the work may have been made by Santafede in a moment of strong interest for chromatic research of Venetian influence i.e. at the end of the first decade of '600. For the preceeding critical attribution cnf. B. MOLAJOLI, op. cit., p. 44 and P. GIUSTI in *Il patrimonio artistico del Banco di Napoli*, Napoli, 1984, p. 10.

[69] Cnf. C. CELANO - G. CHIARINI, op. cit., pp. 750-751; D.A. PARRINO, *Nuova Guida dè Forastieri*, Napoli, 1751, p. 197.

[70] B. MOLAJOLI, op. cit., p. 18; For the *Resurrezione* cnf. also F. FERRANTE, op. cit., p. 30.

[71] Cnf. G. PREVITALI, *La Pittura del Cinquecento...* cit., 1978, p. 121.

[72] Precisely: «Hips. Burghesius pingebat».

[73] For what concerns the figure of Ippolito Borghese cnf. G. PREVITALI, *La pittura del Cinquecento ...*cit., p. 99 and pp. 131-132, n. 12.

[74] For the *Assunzione* and the *Pietà* by Borghese for the *Monte* cnf. F. FERRANTE, op. cit., pp. 32-34 with the preceeding bibliography. The *Assunzione* was finished on 15 november 1603, as it is stated in the document edited by E. NAPPI in this volume.

[75] F. FERRANTE, op. cit., p. 34.

[76] For the Document of 19 february 1601 cnf. M. MORELLI - L. CONFORTI, op. cit., p. 39 and also *Documenti estratti dall'Archivio Storico del Banco di Napoli*, cit., p. 480; for the documents of 20 and 26 February 1601 cnf. the documentary appendix by E. NAPPI in this volume.

[77] Cnf. for instance the drawings *Testa di giovane* nn. 6760 S and 6761 S of the *Gabinetto Disegni e Stampe degli Uffizi* published in V. WITZTHUM, *Cento disegni...* cit., 1967, p. 18.

[78] We are speaking about the payment of 19 October 1601. Cnf. the documentary appendix in this volume; the frescoes of the rooms are attributed to Corenzio by G. SIGISMONDO, op. cit., p. 88; the possibility to identify «la mano di Battistello in alcune sale del Monte» was mentioned by M. STOUGHTON in *La civiltà del Seicento a Napoli*, catalogue of the art exhibition, Napoli, 1984, p. 118; the allegory of *Fecondità* was attributed to Battistello Caracciolo by M. CAUSA PICONE in a lecture made on April 1985 in the auditorium of the museum of *Capodimonte* during the meeting about the Neapolitan civilization of XVII century whose records are being published. The scholar identified Battistello's intervention also in other frescoes of the rooms.

[79] For what concerns the influence of Francesco Curia on some drawings of the young Battistello and for the reconstruction of the beginning and development of the Neapolitan painter's activity cnf. W. PROHASKA, op. cit., pp. 202-204 and pp. 153-268.

[80] Cnf. note 58.

[81] For the documents of 7 July 1736 cnf. the documentary appendix by E. NAPPI in this volume: the documents of payment to Giuseppe Mortale and Pietro Del Po have been published also in V. RIZZO, «Notizie su artisti e artefici dai giornali copiapolizze degli antichi banchi pubblici napoletani», in *Le arti figurative a Napoli nel '700*, Napoli, 1979, p. 234. The monochromatic *Virtù* had been attributed to Giuseppe Bonito also by Ferrante even if with some doubts, cnf. F. FERRANTE, in G.A. GALANTE, *Napoli Sacra*, edited by Nicola Spinosa, Napoli, 1985, p. 149.

[82] For the *Carità* by Bonito cnf. L. GIUSTI, op. cit., p. 120 and N. SPINOSA, *Pittura napoletana del Settecento dal Barocco al Rococò*, Napoli, 1986, p. 169; for the paintings on copper cnf. L. GIUSTI, op. cit., pp. 122-124; for the wooden cupboard cnf. A. PUTATURO MURANO, *Il mobile napoletano del Settecento*, Napoli, 1977, pp. 33, 77-78 and L. GIUSTI, op. cit., p. 122.

[83] Cnf. the document edited by E. NAPPI in the appendix of this volume.

[84] Cnf. note 31 and the paragraph about the chronology of the works.

[85] Cnf. R. RUOTOLO, op. cit., p. 116.

[86] Many thanks to Rosanna Cioffi for her kind suggestions. For the chapel of *Sansevero* cnf. ROSANNA CIOFFI, *La Cappella Sansevero. Arte Barocca e ideologia massonica*, Salerno, 1987, for the painting decoration of the ceiling cnf. R. CIOFFI, op. cit., pp. 63-68.

[87] *Idem*, op. cit., pp. 68-70.

Plastic Decoration

by Maria Ida Catalano

On the elegant façade of the chapel of the *Monte di Pietà*, the presence of the sculptures by Michelangelo Naccherino, Tommaso Montani and Pietro Bernini emphasizes the chromatic taste based on the alternation of «piperno» frames, painted walls and variegated marble backgrounds.

The sculpture of the *Pietà* in the tympanum of the façade is by Naccherino. At the two sides of the sculpture there is a couple of *angeli ploranti* made by Montani. The Pietà is signed at the bottom «Mich Angelus Nacherinus faciebat». It appears to have adjusted itself to the exiguous space of the pediment, lodged «come tra due verticali»[1]. The lateral angels have gestures of peaceful sorrow with which they delicately shatter the limits of the zone that embraces them. The sculptures of the *Carità* and *Sicurità* situated at the sides of the portal were made by Pietro Bernini. The two figures are placed into niches covered with bardiglio slabs, echoing, with their curvilinear rhythms, the concavity of the space.

The ascription of the sculpture to Naccherino and Bernini, already indicated in old Neapolitan guide-books[2], has been later confirmed by documents found in the archives. Thanks to the documents it has also been possible to ascribe the pair of weeping angels to Montani throwing a new light on what was previously disclosed in documents. Some fundamental dates concerning the execution are know from the volume *Conclusioni del Monte*. These few published documents inform us of the essential phases of the work: a payment in June 15th 1600 to Michelangelo Naccherino «purché per tutti luglio prossimo finischi l'opra di marmo della Pietà» and to Pietro Bernini «perché per tutto settembre pross. finischi la Sicurtà» and the settlement on February 9th 1601 at the conclusion of the work when the Marquis of Grottola refused to make an estimate so that «Li Magnifici Gio. Andrea Magliulo e Fabritio Santafede» were called to contemplate the figures. They defined the retribution as adequate once «osservate diligentemente dette statue»[3].

As for the angels by Montani, documents found in the archives state that on December 19th 1603 the sculptor received part of the money due him and, in 1614 the final payment «per li due angeli fatti e posti a sue spese ai lati della Pietà»[4]. Another document, of 1605, which has been already published, speaks of a pair of marble angels commissioned to Montani by the Governors of the *Monte* and refused probably because they did not like them[5]. As a consequence, the actual sculptures are those of 1614, made to replace the 1603 pair, that has been lost.

Even if Tommaso Montani comes from Naccherino's school, he displays more academical tendencies and a more simple classical style. His artistical career is characterised by a certain uniformity of manner far from the significant cultural involvments of Naccherino's production.

The several works the two artists made together[6] lead us to think that Montani worked actively among Naccherino's apprentices who not only worked with marble but also executed models for future realization in metal. This interesting aspect particularly concerned Montani, whose work in this field produced such significant pieces as the silver ciborium of the *Cappella del tesoro di San Gennaro*[7], the ciborium kept in the church of *Santa Patrizia*[8] and, finally, the more important monumental work i.e. the bronzes for the *Cappella del tesoro di San Gennaro*[9].

M. Naccherino, *Pietà*

T. Montani, *Angelo plorante*

The relationship between Naccherino and Bernini is much more complex.
During the first years of XVII century the two sculptors often worked
together in the construction of the *Fontana Medina*[10] , in the Neapolitan
churches of *Gesù Nuovo*[11], *S. Giovanni dei Fiorentini*[12] and in the cathedral of
Amalfi[13]. The importance of their cooperation and their mutual influences
have never been defined in actual, justified judgements but only in some
ephemeral and often discordant annotations which we shall briefly summarise
here.
Maresca had frequently studied Naccherino's style by comparing it to that of
Bernini: more classical and peaceful the former, somewhat unorthodox and
remote from the tradition the latter, who would play a secondary role when
they worked together[14] .
Also in Sobotka's considerations, Naccherino occupies a primary role which is
evident in the use of some sentimental and fantastic typologies of saints, taken
from Bernini[15].
On the contrary, Venturi feels that Naccherino has been strongly influenced
by Bernini's language even if he considers Naccherino's way of expression
«più composto, più contenuto, più conciso»[16].
Morisani considers Naccherino as second-rate and finds Bernini's evident
influence in the slender forms that appear in some of Naccherino's works[16].
Wittkower faces the problem only marginally and affirms that Bernini had to
suffer a process of adjustment to the «clima pietistico della metropoli» of
which Naccherino was an interpreter[18]. Nava Cellini, trying to define the
roles of the two sculptors, speaks of classicism with regard to Naccherino and
of «manierismo estroso» with regard to Bernini since she considered their
aristic experiences as distinct and parallel[19].
According to Parronchi, Bernini's pursuit of airy forms bears witness to the
influence of the older master[20]. The problem of Bernini's formation has been
considered by Negri Arnoldi who regards Naccherino as the possible mediator
between Pietro and the Messina environment where the sculptor took his first
steps[21].
At this point it seemed suitable to face the problem in a different way, taking
advantage of some indications of the critics in an attempt to focalize the
stylistic components of these two sculptors. Although they reveal some
common aspects, their language belongs to different cultural currents.
Parronchi's stimulating considerations[22] about Naccherino induced me to go
back to his origins — full of references to Bandinelli and of «formalismo
michelangiolesco»[23], from which the trend derives to resolve every pathetic
accent in a severe and controlled language.
A new pictorial taste can be seen only when that «nitore imbambolato»
diminishes, that «nitore» which comes to him from Bandinelli and which
dates from his juvenile phase of the *Papireto* river, of the *Nereide* of the
fountain in *Pretoria* Square in *Palermo* (1575-1577) and of the *Tomba di
Alfonso Sanchez* in the Neapolitan church of the *Annunziata* (1588-1589).
In the *Sant'Andrea* which dominates the tomb of Cardinal Gesualdo in the
Cathedral of Naples and in the *Apostoli* in the church of *San Giovanni dei
Fiorentini*, we note a more mobile, more pictorial sensitivity, more aware of
the movements of light.

We can also consider the contemporary bronzes[24], where the influence of Bernini's language is manifest.

This component, however will be essentially marginal in Naccherino's artistic career. His structural vision will be enclosed in the boundaries of a strict and peaceful classicism, to be confirmed in his maturity in works such as the *Monumento funebre ad Ambrogio Salvio* in the Neapolitan church of the *Spirito Santo* (1612-1614) or in the *San Francesco* in the *Cappella del Balzo* in *Santa Chiara* in Naples where the feeling prevails of an absorbed piety.

To this phase belongs also the *Cristo alla Colonna* at *Montelupo Fiorentino* (1616) and the group of *Adamo ed Eva* in *Boboli*'s gardens in Florence (1616) where Bandinelli again represents his preferred landmark.

Defining Bernini's career is more complicated as we have to be content with the little information handed on from various sources.

We know from Baglione's writings that he serves his apprenticeship in Florence with Rodolfo Sirigatti[25] and that later he went with Antonio Tempesta «e con altri pittori di quei tempi al Servitio d'Alessandro Cardinal Farnese in Caprarola» where «varie cose per quel principe dipinse». He then moved to Rome where he devoted himself to the restoration of ancient statues; eventually, again according to Baglione, he arrived in Naples at the age of twenty-two[26].

His first documented works in this city are some restorations and a figure, no longer existing, representing «baccho che fa il moto di spremere l'uva», which the artist executed for Giovanni Antonio Carafa[27].

Further investigation in the archives and some attributed pieces, now completely accepted[28], have allowed us to identify several works carried out later by Bernini during his Neapolitan stay. But there are still many doubts which lead to different suppositions about his stylistic evolution, while some sculptures are still today under discussion. We still do not know the dates of execution of the *Santa Lucia* at *Polistena*, of the relief of the *San Martino che dona il mantello al povero* and of the *Madonna col bambino e San Giovannino* at the Museum of the *Certosa* which is at present again under debate[29].

Ferrari considers this work as a problematic crux, almost an emblem of the unsettled situation in which the studies of seventeenth century Neapolitan sculptures are elaborated[30].

In an attempt to trace the cultural landmarks which could adequately justify the formation of the stylistic language of the artist — on the other hand unmistakable — the critics proposed some theories which have not yet been unified in a clear and definite vision.

Regarding the *Madonna col bambino e San Giovannino* of the *Certosa di San Martino*, Munoz mentioned Sansovino for certain elements of formal grace and purism[31]. Rotondi relates to this point of view since he speaks of Bernini's formation as a derivation of the art of Sansovino filtered trough the Roman works of Ammannati and the Florentine works of Giambologna[32]. The scholar mantains that according to the reading of sources and of some documents, Pietro — documented in Florence in 1595 — collaborated with Giovanbattista Caccini in the execution of the relief of the *Trinità* for the church of *Santa Trinita* in Florence[33].

This conviction gives rise to the supposition of Martinelli who, although accepting the Sansovinian and Tuscan matrix, ascribes to Bernini some works kept in the *Certosa di San Martino* which are characterised by a homogeneus trend towards the rigour of Caccini[34]. Moreover, Martinelli also mentions an influence by Gagini in Bernini's formation, probably absorbed in Southern Italy.

Nava Cellini finds in his expressionistic trend both the influence of the local Neapolitan tradition and the knowledge of Northern art obtained through prints and drawings[35]. Lately, Negri Arnoldi considered fundamental the component of Gagini, together with a mannerism typical of Montorsoli, assimilated by the sculptor in Messina, a city which can be considered the second artistic centre in the South of Italy for sixteenth century sculpture[36]. It seems to me that the events and the contacts regarding the sculptor during the years of his Roman activity have been more carefully analised. In the capital Bernini surely found a richer and more stimulating environment and in fact the influences of Mochi and Mariani are clearly indicated in his works. It is noteworthy that the scholars of the Roman area, especially when they tried to distinguish his work from Gianlorenzo's initial production, insisted on Pietro's mannerism, an element which could seem explicit but which, on the contrary, becomes a characteristic awaiting further research and explanation. A «manierismo estroso» as Nava Cellini defined it which, although reminding us vaguely of Sansovino and of Gagini is substantially far from the classicism of these two sculptors. Neverthless the references to Sansovino and Gagini emphasized by these scholars are not to be eliminated completely. On the contrary, they must be specified philologically in order to avoid vagueness and approximation. As for the sculptor's Neapolitan works, I have already shown my perplexities about the exchanges between Bernini and Caccini — a relation that I would consider inverted in favour of the former. In other words, it seems to me that it was Bernini who influenced Caccini and that the latter briefly diverted his course, otherwise characterised by an «archaeological classicism»[37] in works such as the *Santa Lucia* and the *Santa Agnese* in the *Strozzi* chapel in the church of *Santa Trinita* in Florence. Here the drapery becomes more schematic, constructed through a geometric cut of the levels, with some slight «papery» effects which are usually alien to the sculptor. This last element is, on the contrary, typical of Pietro Bernini since his first works. We can observe it in the *Santa Caterina d'Alessandria* and in the *Santa Lucia* in the church of *San Pietro* at *Morano Calabro* (1591).

It is such a specific and characteristic element as to become a kind of stylistic trademark rather more referable to contemporary pictorial studies than to other contemporary sculptors.

In fact, the language of Girolamo Imparato, an artist of baroque formation — where we find the same papery drapery and a construction of the form through faceting, where the light thickens without creating a spot — has been singled out by Previtali and by Bologna to establish stimulating parallelisms[38]. Bernini's pictorial style — intesified by nervous movements — is evident in his use of chiaroscuro.

Other stylistic components are on the contrary bound to late Tuscan mannerism, such as a certain intellectual way of lingeringly describing complicated coiffures where, crips and wavy, or gathered into thick plaits. The

P. BERNINI, *La Carità*

P. Bernini, *La Carità*, detail

hair creates a play of boundless elegance, revealing a hedonism which had been one of the peculiar elements of that culture.

In the years of his Neapolitan activity, the sculptor represents prevalently holy images, transposing in them elements taken from those mythological representations diffused in the late-manneristic Tuscan culture. In particular, interesting comparisons are suggested by the works of Vincenzo Danti's late phase such as the *Salomé* in the baptisery of Florence or the *Leda* in the Victoria and Albert Museum of London, where, according to a cultural current imposed by Giambologna, a strenuous formalism is pursued, which reaches the most artful and expressive peak in the description of the heads and of the hair[39].

The combination of these factors constitutes the problematic background within which we should consider the sculptures on the façade of the Chapel of the *Monte di Pietà*. In the *Pietà* of Naccherino, the style of Michelangelo undergoes an adjustment to the pietistic and devotional canons of the counter-reformation school. The mantle covers the Virgin's head, but it hides her brow emphasizing the gravity of the figure; the drapery falls amply and embracingly, forming thick folds. The expression on the face of the Virgin reminds us of the Madonnas in the holy groups executed by the sculptor in the same years and based on the same pietism (*Sant'Agata a Castroreale*, near Messina; *Santa Maria della Sanità* and *S. Giovanni a Carbonara* in Naples). The type of Christ-figure evokes the marble *Crocifisso* in the Neapolitan church of the *Spirito Santo* (kept today in the church of *San Carlo all'Arena*) and reveals, in the anatomical study, the influence of Bandinelli. We are reminded, in particular, of the sculptor's Florentine works such as the *Pietà* in the church of *Santacroce* and the *Pietà* in the church of the *Annunziata*.

Though the pair of weeping angels by Montani was made a decade later they have the same pathetic attitude we see in Naccherino's work. The sharply outlined draperies of the two figures reveal a tendency towards geometric solutions probably influenced by Bernini.

The group, as a whole, harmonizes exemplarily with the ideologic charitable and beneficent purposes of the promoters of the *Monte*.

The same intentions are recalled by Bernini's sculptures, beneath which some lines are engraved on marble slabs. Below the *Carità* we read the following words in couplets: «Forsān abest misero signata pecunia civi/Atque illum interēa tēpora saeva premunt/Nūmorū huic operi ingētes cumulamus acervos/Pignore deposito, quod petit inde damus» referring to the possibility of borrowing on pledge at the *Monte*; nearly, below the *Sicurtà* we read: «Si quis amat brevibus cauto persolvere chartis/Aut timet insidias furis, et arma domi./Congerite huc aurū, placidos, et carpite soños/Per me securis civibus esse licet» where explicit reference is made to the security of depositing valuables in the safes of the *Monte*[40]. The foregoing makes it clear that the façade had been conceived as a kind of manifesto where purposes and programmes were expressed in an instructive spirit, typical of the counter-reformation. But, in spite of the thematic subordination, the sculptures of Pietro Bernini do not exhaust their formal significance.

Compared to Naccherino, whose language is more functional in the pietistic climate of the moment, Bernini is not able to hide completely those slightly

P. Bernini, *La Sicurtà*

P. BERNINI, *La Sicurtà*, detail

aesthetical cultural components of a manneristic style. In the *Carità* the slightly arched figure is balanced by the widing chain of children's frail bodies. In spite of his pietistic intentions, the sculptor lovingly describes the crisp hair of the woman tied up in thick plaits. The faces of the children are represented with an expressionistic taste pervaded with a slight restlessnes.

In the *Sicurtà* the slight twisting favours the sentimental attitude of the figure: the body twists slightly on the left leg, the head bent on the right arm, leans against the column[41]. The movement, only slightly accentuated, is favoured by the linear play of the drapery fringed with great virtuosity.

Subtle harmonies equilibrate the image some details reveal the manneristic matrix: the extreme elegance of the coiffure, the cartilaginous aspect of the buckle decorating the dress[42].

Some formal references to late Tuscan mannerism, of Giambologna derivation, are again required but it is to be pointed out that the assimilation of the canons of the great Flemish artist among his contemporary sculptors was a complicated and variegated phenomenon which critics have not yet focalized.

A particular stylistic moment of Giambologna's career is connected with our subject: I refer to these sculptures executed for the *Grimani* chapel in the church of the *Castelletto* in Genoa, which were realized when the artist chose, as many did and we do not know how honestly, a chaster and more devout language which was convincing in a different way[43].

Schmidt mentioned the Genoese sculptures (whose models according to the scholar existed in Florence) in reference to the *Temperanza* by Giovan Battista Caccini, standing today in the Metropolitan Museum of New York[44].

We have already spoken of the difference between the language of Caccini and of Bernini; but we cannot exclude that the two sculptors, though through different formal values, both referred to that moment of evolution in Giambologna's career.

We do not intend, with this analysis, to exhaust all the references present in Bernini's work, but, on the contrary, we do intend to offer some suggestions which may shed light on his complex culture.

There are still several problems concerning the interpretation of the sculptures in the Chapel of the *Monte di Pietà*. The *Carità* has been compared with the problematic *Madonna col Bambino e San Giovannino* of the *San Martino* Museum and with the *San Matteo* of the church of the *Gesù Nuovo*[45].

But, apart from these purely compositive comparisons, in the sculptures of the *Monte di Pietà* Bernini expresses himself with a more significant and explicit language in comparison with the works he carries out in those same years: I refer to the *San Matteo* in the *Gesù Nuovo* and to the *Santi Bartolomeo e Simone* of the *Gerolamini*. His geometrical trend and his nervous way of handling the form to sharpen the profiles are accentuated in the *Carità* and in the *Sicurtà*.

It is most likely, however, that following cleaning — and removal of the dirt — the shaded passagges will appear softer, attenuating, if only partially the contrast with the other contemporary works.

Today a few elements remain of the marble decoration inside the chapel of the *Monte di Pietà* as Giovan Battista Cavagna, Roman architect, had conceived it at the beginning of the 17th century. The high altar

Little choir (sec. XVII)

— transformed, as we shall see, in the 18th century — at present is embodied in a mural aggregate of architectural elements attributable to the initial 17th century construction. The architrave in white marble and violet breccia, the delicately carved Corinthian capitals, the alveolate columns in antique green marble [46] on tall plinths, the moulded frame surrounding the *Deposizione* by Fabrizio Santafede are seen as elements of an ornamental, late-manneristic repertory which, at the beginning of the 17th century, anticipate further, prolific developments in the novelty of their chromatic values.

The marble floor of the presbyterial area emphasizes the persistence of a flooring different from the majolica which took its place in the 18th century. The square of antique yellow, violet breccia and antique green geometric designs recalling the numerous inlaid marble tables so prevalent in the furnishings of Neapolitan churches between the end of the 16th and the beginning of the 17th century [47]. Archival documents confirm that the drawing of this early flooring was executed by Cavagna in 1603 [48].

I feel that the drawing of the four small choir stalls situated in the corners of the chapel dates back to this same phase of the works, recalling the drawing of the entrance portal executed in variegated marble. The severe essentiality of the marble frames on the door-posts and the elegant balustrades still indicate 16th century taste, while a later date must be given to the addition of marble consoles richly decorated with mock triglyphs in inlaid marble, pairs of grinning masks and acanthus leaves [49]. The four doors located near the four choir stalls have door-posts and architraves of variegated marble — white and bluish bardiglio marble for the two doors near the entrance and peacock-blue Carrara marble for the other two doors leading to the halls of the Congregation and to the anteroom of the sacristy. The four doors were all restored in XVIII century [50].

Prior to the 18th century restorations the *Memoria del Cardinale Acquaviva*, by Cosimo Fanzago [51] had been part of the furnishings of the chapel; it was later removed to the anteroom of the sacristy. According to 17th century sources it was situated below the painting by Fabrizio Santafede, Sigismondo being the first to mention it as being in the sacristy [52]. Archival documentation allows us to establish for certain the year in which the trasference occurred. In 1730 the marble-cutter Carlo Tucci was paid to shift the *Memoria Acquaviva*, its place to be occupied by a new altar [53].

According to documents, on that occasion Tucci also executed «il piedistallo», to be identified by the moulded border in white marble and Spanish «broccatello» forming the base of the monument.

The *Memoria Acquaviva* is made up of two distinct sections, the upper part formed by an inscribed tablet surrounded by a fascia in Spanish «broccatello» and a framework of mixed lines; on top is a cardinal's hat trimmed with two tasselled cords which fall across a cartouche, creating a lively play of decorative movement. Two torch-bearing putti at either side, placed above a moulded fascia in white marble, form a pleasing combination with the volutes below, linking the two sections together. The lower part consists of two monumental supporting columns in the form of male figures, back to back, correlated by a drapery passing through the mouth of a lion whose head, between the two figures, separates the imposing scene [54].

C. Fanzago, *Memoria del Cardinale Ottavio Acquaviva*

Cardinal Ottavio Acquaviva d'Aragona (Naples 1560-1612) was one of the most prominent figures in Naples during the Counter-Reformation, actively endeavouring to diffuse the rules of the Council of Trent in that city and engaging himself in several important charitable initiatives[55]. We read in the dedicatory inscription that he contributed the sum of 20,000 ducats to further the construction of the *Monte di Pietà*.

According to archival documentation there were payments to Cosimo Fanzago dating from 1617 to 1618 for «l'epitaffio di marmo... dell'Illustrissimo Cardinale Acquaviva»[56]. These were the initial years of activity in Naples for the sculptor from Bergamo, busying himself in the workshop of the marble-cutter Angelo Landi[57]. Among the works surviving from this youthful period are the *Stemmi* (coats of arms) for the *Palazzo degli Studi* (1615-1616)[58], the *Lavamano* (wash-stand) in the sacristy of the church of the *Rifugio* and the *Sant'Ignazio* (1616) for the church of *Gesù*, in Catanzaro, at present in the *Marincola Cattaneo* chapel of the cemetery in this city — all making persuasive references to the local late-manneristic production[59].

An entirely different approach is seen, however, when we consider the *Telamones* (supporting columns in the form of male figures) of the *Memoria Acquaviva*, the small bronze figures of St. Peter and St. Paul executed for the ciborium of the church of *Santa Patrizia*, the sculptures in the Borrello chapel of the church of *Gesù Nuovo* and the *Portrait of Geronimo Flerio* in the church of *Santa Maria di Costantinopoli*. In a careful study rich in stylistic comparisons, and prompted by preceding critical observations, Aurora Spinosa has found reference points to Fanzago's eloquence in the Lombard sculptors Annibale Fontana and Galeazzo Alessi[60]. Nevertheless, both the particular observance of cultural aspects as well as the stimulating revival of Lombard traditions — which seem to give rise to a more personal and lively expression — remain problematical when we take account of the brief span of time in which the cited works were executed.

The ornamental phrasing of the *Memoria Acquaviva* is still inspired by local late-manneristic traditions. The design of the tablet is analogous to the one in the monument by Michele Gentile senior found in the cathedral at Barletta. The cardinal's hat motif, with its tasseled cords, was widely used as a decorative feature between the late 16th and early 17th centuries in the coats of arms placed at the entrance to the chapels or at the sides of numerous funeral monuments. In the curvilinear flow of the two slender volutes situated below the tablet, the figure of a tiny monster reveals a typically manneristic taste. The torch-bearing putti recall similar ones standing at the sides of the monument to *Geronimo Flerio* in the church of *S. Maria di Costantinopoli*[61] but, unlike the latter, they reveal an intention to enliven the form by their slight twisting gesture.

In the lower part, the head of a lion — holding a drapery between his teeth — recalls in a more naturalistic manner a theme already used in late 16th century decoration; for instance, it can be found on the sarcophagus of the funeral monument to Paolo Spinelli situated in the church of *Santo Spirito*. As for the telamone figures, reference has been made to classical influences[62] and to a vigour after the manner of Michelangelo visible in the powerful articulation of the postures[63]. We are dealing here with cultural components typical of a manneristic conception which will accompany the sculptor's work for years to come. Spinosa[64] recognizes in the telamones an emergence of elements of Lombard culture in the intense expressive vigour, the strong realism and sensitive luminosity. The telamone motif will be taken up again by the sculptor, and varied, i.e. in the entrance stairway to the church of *Trinità delle Monache* as terminals of the balustrade and in the *Sebeto* fountain where, transformed into powerful figures of Tritons, they enrich the decorative theme.

The elements under analysis here remained substantially unaltered for more than a century. A new wave of decorative interventions, began to be seen only after the beginning of the 18th century, greatly transforming the image of the Chapel and up-dating it to coincide with the taste of the new time. In the first half of the 18th century the situation of the Banks in Naples was still to be considered prosperous even though one could speak no longer of their time-honoured original opulence.

During the period of the Austrian reign and later with the Bourbons the banks continued to carry out fundamentally the function of financing the royal court and the city. As for the *Monte di Pietà*, we learn from Filangieri that «Il continuo crescer delle opere costrinse il Monte ad ampliare la propria sede» with the purchase, in 1728, of the adjacent house of Don Francesco de Laurentiis and, in 1748, of the nearby house of Don Domenico Antonio de Palma[65]. Moreover, we know that in 1731 the Bank of the *Monte di Pietà* granted a loan of 20,000 ducats to the Court. Consequently, in spite of the difficulties which had characterized the vice-royalty years, the economic situation of this institution was still flourishing. Indeed, we can speak of a definite decline only in the years beginning with the second half of the 18th century[66].

We do not know the specific reasons which induced the deputies of the *Monte di Pietà*, in 1700, to undertake a programme of reconstruction and decorative embellishment. However, this is doubtlessly one of the elements which indirectly confirm the economic prosperity of the Bank.

The works of reconstruction began with the altar by the marble worker Gaetano Sacco (1716) which is below the painting of *Assunta* by Ippolito Borghese[67]. We may infer from documentation that only the inlaid marble background — against which the altar was to be placed — is still existent. We also learn that in 1729 and in 1730, another altar — below the painting of *Resurrezione* by Fabrizio Santafede — was made by the marble-worker Carlo Tucci on the drawing by Bartolomeo Granucci[68].

Further documentation shows that in the same years the «vecchio altare» i.e. that of 1716 was transformed «a somiglianza del nuovo». Since the two marble altars flanking the chapel are very much alike, we can presume that rather than transform the old altar a new one was made. From 1748 till 1778 documents mention repairs and embellishments to the high attar[69]. 18th century rennovations are recognizable in the tabernacle and the tiered reliquary in the decorative elements supporting the altar — a variegated marble version of the motifs present in the two white altars — and in the altar-frontal which repeats the theme of crown of laurel and cross done in bronze on a background of green Calabria marble. The side altars designed by Granucci are simpler and more elegant, with their decorative reliquaries adorned with cherub and a continuous frieze of acanthus leaves. The subtle shell volutes beneath the altar harmonize perfectly with the sober, linear cadence; the extreme simplicity of the frontal is decorated with a white crown of laurel encircling a design of the cross, the single chromatic element in inlaid marble. Granucci has been relegated to the sphere of classicist trends toward late-baroque and rococo[70], fundamentally considered a decorator and advocate of fashionable themes[71]. In the altars of the *Monte di Pietà* the artist seems to utilize an inclination towards themes of Sanfelice, remote from the late baroque solution of altars in inlaid marble with naturalistic motifs. There are, in fact, certain drawings attributed to San Felice which remind us, in their simplicity, solutions adopted by Granucci[72]. In my opinion, what particularly qualifies the altars in the chapel of the *Monte di Pietà* is the rather singular fact that they have been done in white marble[73].

The cherub heads adorning them, particularly the lateral ones, reveal appreciable sculptural skill in the subtle pictorial style, in the taste for soft and shaded surfaces. Borrelli includes them in the Register of Matteo Bottiglieri[74]. In the anteroom of the sacristy, the *lavabo*, or sacerdotal wash basin, represents another episode realized in 18th century interventions. It was made in order to replace the one realized by Angelo Landi (1614) mentioned in the documents[75]. Already in the 17th century, with the tendency towards ornamental liturgical vestments, the sacerdotal lavabo became one of the favourite themes of the new baroque taste seen in Neapolitan churches. The white and bardiglio marble *lavabo* of Cosimo Fanzago in the sacristy of the church of the *Certosa di San Martino* constitutes the first interpretation in a monumental key providing the most varied and bizarre inventions along the course of the 17th and successive centuries. In the same *Certosa*, the *lavabo* which Tagliacozzi Canale planned for the small cloister of the refectory (1722-1724) represents one of the culminating points along this course. In the lavabo of the *Monte di Pietà* the continuous play of curves and contrasting volutes reveals a typical «rocaille» taste. According to the documents found in the archives, it was made 1743 by the marble worker Carlo Adamo[76].

Deserving particular consideration is the wood group *Pietà con Angeli Ploranti* to be seen in the chapel. Its original location is not known, but it was found in the store-rooms of the *Monte* by Morelli and Conforti[77] and commented on by Causa in the catalogue of the art-exhibition «Sculture lignee in Campania»[78].

On that occasion, certain sculptures preserved in Neapolitan churches — dated between the end of the 16th and the beginning of the 17th century and characterized by a common refinement of Iberian inspiration — were published for the first time.

Making reference to the 18th century biographer De Dominici[79], Causa confronts the problem of the sculptor Francesco Mollica from a critical point of view. According to De Dominici, Mollica was the author of the wood group in the church of *Gesù Nuovo* representing *Crocifisso e dolenti*. In considering Mollica a pupil of Naccherino, De Dominici created a link between this still obscure personality and the Tuscan master who had worked in Naples for over thirty years. Causa alluded to this tie-up even more

B. Granucci, C. Tucci, side-altar

C. Adamo, Sacerdotal lavabo

CASTILIAN SCULPTOR (beginning of XVIII century), *Pietà*

CASTILIAN SCULPTOR (beginning of XVIII century), *Pietà*, detail

CASTILIAN SCULPTOR (beginning of XVIII century), *Angelo plorante*

distinctly, but singled out the Iberian influence as the most notable
characteristic of the sculpture in *Gesù Nuovo*[80]. Other pieces collocated by
Causa in the Iberian-inspired sphere were the two *dolenti* in the church of
SS. Filippo and Giacomo, the *Crocifisso e Vergine dolente* in the church of the
Incoronata — attributed specifically to Naccherino and his workshop — and
the *Pietà con angeli ploranti* in the chapel of the *Monte di Pietà*. Contrarily,
Causa retained the two exemplars representing the *Angelo Custode* coming
from the churches of *San Domenico Maggiore* and *Gesù Nuovo*[81] to stem from
a manneristic culture, more closely bound to the examples of local painting.
Later critics had not faced the problem of this group of works in its entirety
until Borrelli, in 1970[82] — in a note in the chapter on Neapolitan wooden
sculpture in the 17th century — touched on the question again, briefly offering
further motives for consideration. This scholar made additions to the still
fragmentary catalogue dealing with wooden sculpture between the 16th and
17th centuries, emphasizing more precisely the Iberian roots of the majority
of these pieces. In the *Gesù Nuovo* group, Borrelli singled out a direct
derivation from the school of Valladolid, and in the *Pietà con angeli ploranti*
in the chapel of the *Monte* he proferred close ties with a work on the same
subject conserved in Valladolid in the chapel of the *Sette dolori*. No longer,
then, local products influenced by the Iberian school — as Causa asserted —
but works by Spanish artists, either sent from Spain or actually executed in
Naples. The same opinion has recently been aired by Roberto Middione who,
while placing again under the name of Mollica the group of works cited by
Causa — which, in my opinion, seem to have different stylistic
characteristics[83] — has removed from the Naccherino catalogue the *Crocifisso*
in the church of the *Incoronata*, today in *Santa Maria di Costantinopoli* at
Cappella Cangiani, agreeing with the writer concerning the different source of
the works of the Tuscan master, marked by a counter-reformistic pietism
characterized by the powerful influence of «formalismo michelangiolesco»[84].
As for the wood group in the *Monte di Pietà*, we agree with Middione who
has pointed out «nell'accesa policromia, nell'intaglio profondo, nella
drammatica espressività» the stylistic features of a Spanish artist who was
formed in Castile, at the school of Vallodolid, and influenced by Italian
culture — recognizable, in particular, by the composite order of the group.
In this connection we should consider that the pyramidal pattern after the
manner of Michelangelo, infused with preceding Flemish and German
influences, had been successful in Spain. In Castile, where «romanismo
michelangiolesco» had been a decisive factor, the Toledan sculptor Bautista
Vazquez realized, in 1561, a marble replica of the Roman *Pietà* (Cathedral of
Avila) which was to become an important point of reference to local
sculptors. The theme of the *Pietà* was later modified in Spain at the beginning
of the 17th century by Gregorio Fernandes who, in his wood group in the
Museum of Sculpture at Valladolid, broke away from the pyramidal pattern,
constructing a diagonal composition with the Virgin holding on one knee the
body of Christ, arching towards the ground.
The chestnut wood group in the *Monte di Pietà* was later stuccoed and
painted. The back of the group, rough-hewn and unpainted, still shows traces
of gouge and chisel strokes. The «estofados» technique imitates the design of

brocade fabrics in a number of different methods, i.e. for the veil of the Virgin, a rhomboidal network is painted in gold on a ochre base with the tip of the paintbrush while on her mantle green and carmine red decorative motifs stands out from a gold background. The lively chromatic effect is emphasized by a shiny varnish completely covering the painted parts. The body of Christ lying across the Virgin's knee is painted in a bluisch leaden colour furrowed with drops of blood. The anonymous sculptor has insisted on anatomical detail, outlining the nude body of Christ, barely covered by a cloth, with tense muscles and swollen abdomen. The wood is worked with aggressiveness and a lively plastic sense — characteristics which recall artists like Francisco de Ricon, in whose circle the initial formation of Gregorio Fernandez most likely occurred.

[1] A. Venturi, «La Scultura del Cinquecento», in *Storia dell'Arte Italiana*, Milano, 1936, X, part. II, p. 594.

[2] C. Celano, *Notizie del Bello dell'Antico e del Curioso della città di Napoli*, edited by G.B. Chiarini, Napoli, 1856-1860, II, pp. 925, 1152; P. Sarnelli, *Guida de' forestieri... della città di Napoli*, Napoli, 1697, p. 212; D.A. Parrino, *Nuova guida de' forestieri*, Napoli, 1725, p. 191; G. Sigismondo, *Descrizione della città di Napoli e i suoi borghi*, 1788-1789, II, p. 89; G.A. Aspreno Galante, *Guida sacra della città di Napoli*, Napoli, 1872, p. 205.

[3] A. Maresca di Serra Capriola, *Sulla vita e sulle opere di Michelangelo Naccherino*, Napoli, 1890, pp. 52-53; E. Tortora, *Nuovi documenti per la Storia del Banco di Napoli*, Napoli, 1890, p. 37; G. Filangieri, *Documenti per la storia, le arti e le industrie delle province napoletane*, V, Napoli, 1891, p. 419; M. Morelli-L. Conforti, *La Cappella del Monte di Pietà*, in the building of the same name belonging to Banco di Napoli, Napoli, 1899, pp. 21-24; «Documenti estratti dall'Archivio Storico del Banco di Napoli...», in *Rassegna Economica*, X, 1940, p. 325; F. Strazzullo, «Documenti per la Storia dell'Arte del '600 a Napoli» in *Atti dell'Accademia Pontaniana*, XXVIII, 1979, p. 325.

[4] Cnf. the documents n. 18-20 in the Appendix.

[5] «Documenti estratti...», cit., 1940, p. 266.

[6] In Naples the two artists worked together on several occasions: *Fontana Medina, Cappella Fornaro*, in the church of *Gesù Nuovo, Monumento funebre del Cardinal Gesualdo* in the Cathedral and *Fontana di Santa Lucia* (Cnf. in the «Regesti» the items «Tommaso Montani» and «Michelangelo Naccherino» edited by M.I. Catalano, in *Civiltà del Seicento a Napoli*, catalogue of the art-exhibition, 1984, II, pp. 215-216, 220-221).

[7] A. Maresca, *Sulla vita e sulle opere...*, cit., 1890, pp. 58-60; G.B. D'Addosio, «Documenti inediti di artisti napoletani del XVI e XVII secolo», in *Archivio Storico per le Province Napoletane*, XLII, 1917, p. 114; E. and C. Catello, *La Cappella del Tesoro di San Gennaro*, Napoli, 1977, pp. 55, 93-94.

[8] G.B. D'Addosio, *Documenti...*, cit., 1916, p. 157; *ivi*, 1920, p. 243; *Documenti estratti...*, cit., 1940, p. 266.

[9] The deputies of the *Cappella del Tesoro di San Gennaro* commissioned a series of monumental bronzes by Montani and the two artists from Vicenza, Cristofaro and Gian Domenico Monterosso. The three artists executed only three of them: *S. Attanasio, S. Gennaro, S. Aspreno*. There is still some question (F. Capobianco, cit., Napoli, 1984, pp. 216-217) about the attribution of the single sculptures.

[10] Naccherina and Bernini worked at the *Fontana Medina* during the years 1600-1601 (cnf. A. Maresca, *op. cit.*, pp. 51-52; A. Colombo, «La Fontana Medina», in *Napoli Nobilissima*, VI, 1897, pp. 65-70; G. Sobotka, «Pietro Bernini» in *L'Arte*, XII, 1909; p. 404). The statue of *Nettuno* and the group of satyres have been ascribed to Naccherino; according to a document quoted by Sobotka, Bernini also worked at these statues. Moreover, this artist executed also four sea-monsters later identified in the dolphins ridden by «putti», at present damaged by uncareless restoration. The fountain presents several analogies with that of *Orione* executed in Messina by Montorsoli and with the *Fontana Pretoria* executed in Palermo by Camillani. It recalls the typical structure «a candelabro», with a division in several sections, articulated around a vertical central axis. In particular, the *Fontana Medina* resembles that of *Orione* in the central shaped basin, decorated with masks. When considering the work as a whole, the successive intervention by Fanzago, mentioned by Cantone, cannot but be considered (G. Cantone, *Napoli Barocca e Cosimo Fanzago*, Napoli, 1984, p. 413-418).

[11] In the *Cappella Fornaro*, in the church of *Gesù Nuovo*, Naccherino did the *Sant'Andrea* (signed and dated 1601) that had been commissioned in 1600 (cnf. G.B. D'Addosio, *Documenti inediti di artisti napoletani*, op. cit., 1917, p. 112). On the contrary, Bernini did the *San Matteo* that, thanks to some recent studies (E. Nappi, «Le chiese dei Gesuiti a Napoli» in *Seicento napoletano. Arte, costume, ambiente*, edited by Roberto Pane, Molano, 1984, p. 336, document 53) can be dated 1601. According to me, the *Sant'Andrea* by Naccherino resembles the statue of *San Jacopo* by Montorsoli, made for the tomb of Jacopo Sannazzaro in the Neapolitan church of *Santa Maria del Parto*.

[12] Documentation tells us that the group of sculptures in the church of *San Giovanni dei Fiorentini*, moved in 1950 to the *Incoronata madre del Buon Consiglio*, was made by Naccherino and his apprentices. In this regard, we lack any archival document: we are only sure about the date of execution of the *San Giacomo* by Francesco Cassano (1610) (G.B. D'Addosio, op. cit., 1921, p. 390). Rotondi ascribed one of the two sculptures to Pietro Bernini (P. Rotondi, «Studi intorno a Pietro Bernini» in *Rivista del Real Istituto d'Archeologia e Storia dell'Arte*, V, 1935-1936, First part, p. 189) and precisely the *Sant'Andrea* presumably executed during the first years of 1600 because of the strong analogies with the statues of *San Bartolomeo* and *San Simone* in the church of *Gerolomini*. For what concerns the iconographie interpretation of the sculptures in *San Giovanni dei Fiorentini*, I think I have suggested a new interpretation connecting them with the *Apostolato* by Montorsoli in the Cathedral of Messina (M.I. Catalano, «Scultori toscani a Napoli alla fine del Cinquecento. Considerazioni e problemi», in *Storia dell'arte*, 54, 1985, pp. 123-132). An *Apostolato* had been planned for the Cathedral of Orvieto as well. Giovan Battista Caccini had contributed to it with the statue of *San Giacomo Maggiore* bearing his signature and the date 1591. This may suggest new hints for the interpretation of

Neapolitan sculptures. I have some doubts about one of the figures of the Apostles ascribed to Naccherino both by previous critics and by myself: I refer to the bald Apostle reminding me particulary Bandinelli's style (O. Morisani, *Saggi sulla scultura napoletana del '500*, Napoli, 1941, p. 53; M.I. Catalano, *Scultori toscani a Napoli*, op. cit., p. 126) different from the others owing to a more academic and archaelogical style. These elements lead me to think of a direct intervention by Caccini. Until now Caccini's presence in Naples has been a mere hypothesis but according to these considerations is now more well-founded.

[13] In the crypt of Amalfi Cathedral, Naccherino executed the bronze sculpture of *Sant'Andrea* and Bernini the two marble sculptures of *Santo Stefano e San Lorenzo* (1602).

[14] A. Maresca, *op. cit.*, p. 14.

[15] G. Sobotka, *op. cit.*, p. 409, 412.

[16] A. Venturi, *op. cit.*, p. 601.

[17] O. Morisani, *op. cit.*, pp. 52-54; O. Morisani, «La scultura del '500 a Napoli», in *Storia di Napoli*, Cava dei Tirreni, 1972, V., pp. 719-780.

[18] R. Wittkower, *Art and Architecture in Italy 1600 to 1750*, Harmondsworth, 1958, Reccomendend italian edition Torino, 1972, p. 109.

[19] A. Nava Cellini, «La Scultura dal 1610 al 1656», in *Storia di Napoli*, Cava dei Tirreni, 1972, p. 783; A. Nava Cellini, *La scultura del '600*, Torino, 1982, p. 117.

[20] A. Parronchi, «Sculture e progetti di Michelangelo Naccherino», in *Prospettiva*, 1980, p. 34.

[21] F. Negri Arnoldi, «Due Schede ed una ipotesi per Pietro Bernini giovane», in *Bollettino d'Arte*, LXVIII, 1983, p. 16. On the occasion, the scholar informed us about the important discovery of the sculpture of *Santa Lucia* kept in the church of *Immacolata di Polistena*. With this discovery Negri Arnoldi added another element about the juvenile production of the sculptor. In the same essay, he eliminated from the artist's works the sculptures by Terranova Sappo Minulio, ascribed to Bernini by Martinelli (V. Martinelli, «Contributi alla scultura del Seicento. Pietro Bernini e figli», in *Commentari*, 1953, p. 135). On the contrary, in my opinion, the attribution to Bernini of the *Santa Caterina d'Alessandria* in the church of *San Francesco a Barcellona* near Messina is not well-founded (Negri Arnoldi, *op. cit.*, p. 106).

[22] A. Parronchi, «Resti del Presepe di Santa Maria Novella», in *Antichità viva*, 1965, 3, p. 15.

[23] M.I. Catalano, «Michelangelo Naccherino» in *Civiltà del Seicento a Napoli*, catalogue of the art-exhibition, Napoli, 1984, vol. II; M.I. Catalano, *Scultori toscani a Napoli...*, op. cit., p. 124. Martinelli (V. Martinelli, *Manierismo, Barocco, Rococò. Nella scultura italiana*, Milano, 1979, p. 8) underlined a tendency to plastic chiaroscuro and to the relief of the naked figures in what is commonly defined «fomalismo michelangiolesco». According to him, this particulars are common to the works made in Florence and in Rome where Michelangelo's sculptural technique was associated with accademical tendencies. Recently, Francesco Abbate, underlined the relations between Naccherino and Neapolitan sculpture, while, according to me, these relations are not particulary important (F. Abbate, «La decorazione scultorea della Cappella Montalto nella chiesa napoletana di Santa Maria del Popolo agli Incurabili», in *Antichità viva*, XXIV, 1985, 1-2-3, pp. 138-144).

[24] Naccherino made some monumental bronze sculptures: *Sant'Andrea*, Amalfi Cathedral (1602-1604), *San Matteo*, Salerno Cathedral (1606) and the *monumento funebre a Fabrizio Pignatelli*, chapel of *Santa Maria Materdomini* (1596-1607). Also the little bronze sculpture *Battesimo di Cristo* (1619-1621), above the font in the Cathedral of Naples, should be attributed to the Naccherino-Montani school.

[25] G. Baglione, *La vita de' pittori, scultori ed architetti dal pontificato di Gregorio XIII del 1592 infino a' tempi di Papa Urbano VIII nel 1642*, Roma, 1642, p. 304.

[26] G. Baglione, *op. cit.*, p. 305.

[27] G. Ceci, «Per la biografia degli artisti del XVI e XVII secolo. Nuovi documenti II. Scultori», in *Napoli Nobilissima*, 1906, p. 117.

[28] With the recent publication of the documents attesting to the payment for the *Vita attiva* (1596) the Monastery of San Martino commissioned to Bernini (M.I. Catalano, *op. cit.*, p. 129) and of the *San Matteo* (1601) made by the sculptor for the church of *Gesù* in Naples (E. Nappi, *op. cit.*, p. 336) two other elements have been added to the reconstruction of Bernini's Neapolitan activity. Critics have confirmed only the attribution to Bernini of the *Sant'Andrea* of the church of *San Giovanni dei Fiorentini* (P. Rotondi, *Studi intorno...* op. cit., p. 197). The *San Martino che dona il mantello al povero* of the Museum of *San Martino* (V. Martinelli, *Contributi...*, op. cit., p. 139) and the *Santa Lucia* of the church of *Immacolata di Polistena* (F. Negri Arnoldi, *op. cit.*, p. 103).

[29] Capobianco has reconstructed the complicated but fortunate criticism this work has received. The critic has also edited the biography and the chronological history of the artist on the occasion of the art-exhibition *Civiltà del Seicento a Napoli* (cnf. F. Capobianco, *op. cit.*, Napoli 1984, p. 157). Recently Catello has come back to the subject (E. Catello, «Nota sulla Madonna del Museo di San Martino» in *Napoli Nobilissima*, n.s., XXIII, 1984, pp. 111-112) and thanks to the discovery of an important document he has been able to trow new light on the matter. The scholar thinks that the group has been executed by Bernini alone in contrast with those who think that the sculpture of San Martino is the result of a collaboration between two artists. Mormone commented the study of Catello with a brief note (p. 113). He considers the group from a 17th century point of view, traceable to certain stylistic features diffused between Rome and Naples in the first half of the 17th century. I have considered the work as strongly charachterised by a Manneristic culture linked to Pietro Bernini (M.I., Catalano, *Scultori toscani a Napoli...*, op. cit., 1985, p. 131.

[30] O. Ferrari, *I grandi momenti della scultura e della decorazione plastica*, op. cit., Napoli, 1984, p. 145.

[31] A. Munoz, *Il padre del Bernini: Pietro Bernini scultore (1562-1629)*, in *Vita d'Arte*, IV, 1909, p. 428.

[32] I think that if the reference to Giambologna is pertinent — and we shall see later how it should be interpreted — we must exclude the reference to Ammannati because his academical treatment of the surfaces is accompanied by the research of studies tonalites that mitigate, as Dupré pointed out, (M.G. Ciardi Dupré, «La prima attività dell'Ammannati scultore», in *Paragone*, 135, 1961, pp. 3-28) in a classicistic direction, the subtle liberties of his mannerism, connected with Venetian experiences, particulary in his Roman works.

[33] P. Rotondi, «Educazione artistica di Pietro Bernini», in *Capitolium*, 1933, p. 397. The hypotesis of a collaboration between Bernini and Caccini in the work of the relief of *Santa Trinita* has been attenuated by Schmidt (J.K. Schmidt, *Studien zum statuarischen Werk des Giovanni Battista Caccini*, Munchen, 1971, pp. 156-158).

[34] V. Martinelli, *Contributi...*, op. cit., p. 135. I think we have to exclude from the works attributed to Bernini by Martinelli the so-called *Purità*, then identified as *Vita Contemplativa*. I believe it should be attributed to Caccini himself for the strong analogies with the *Temperanza* of the Metropolitan Museum of New York.

[35] A. Nava Cellini, *La scultura dal 1610...*, op. cit., 1972, p. 783; A. Nava Cellini, *La scultura...*, op. cit., 1982, p. 22.

[36] F. Negri Arnoldi, op. cit., p. 107.

[37] M.I. Catalano, *Scultori toscani a Napoli*, op. cit., p. 128.

[38] G. Previtali, «Dalla venuta di Teodoro D'Errico (1574) a quella di Michelangelo da Caravaggio» (chap. III), in *Storia di Napoli*, V, Cava dei Tirreni, 1972, p. 879; F. Bologna, *Text of the University lessons of the accademical year 1975-1976*; G. Previtali, *La pittura del Cinquecento a Napoli e nel vicereame*, Torino, 1978, p. 114. Parallels are established most of all with the painting by Imparato *Assunzione della Vergine* (1603), on the ceiling of the church of *Santa Maria La Nova*. But in *Gesù tra i dottori* of *Santa Maria de la Vid* in Burgos we can already see the evolution of Imparato's language towards Barrocci's style (P.L. Leone de Castris, op. cit., in *Il patrimonio artistico del Banco di Napoli*, Napoli, 1984, p. 12). For what concerns Bernini, Barrocci's influence can be seen in the chromatic research, influenced as it is also by Northern elements (in the sharpene nervous drawing) as Nava Cellini pointed out. We have also to add that only later, during his Roman years, his pictorial art will be transformed under Venetian influence.

[39] H. Keutner, «The Palazzo Pitti Venus and others works by Vincenzo Danti», in *The Burlington Magazine*, 1958, Dec., pp. 427-431.

[40] R. Filangieri, *I banchi di Napoli. Dalle origini alla costituzione del Banco delle due Sicilie (1539-1808)*, Napoli, 1940, pp. 42-43.

[41] C. Ripa, *Iconologia del Cavalier Cesare Ripa Perugino. Notabilmente accresciuta d'immagini, di Annotazioni e di fatti dell'Abate Cesare Orlandi*, Perugia, V, 1767, pp. 161-162.

[42] A similar motif decorates the vest of the *Vita Attiva* of the church of the *Certosa di San Martino* (cnf. M.I. Catalano, *Scultori toscani a Napoli...*, op. cit., p. 130).

[43] L. Berti, *Il principe dello studiolo*, Firenze, 1967, p. 178.

[44] J.K. Schmidt, op. cit., p. 23.

[45] P. Rotondi, *Studi intorno...*, op. cit., p. 196; F. Capobianco, op. cit., Napoli, 1984, p. 157.

[46] For what concerns the identification of the precious marbles decorating the chapel, I consulted the following texts: M. Pieri, *I marmi d'Italia*, Milano, 1964; R. Gnoli, *Marmora Romana*, Roma, 1971.

[47] For instance a similar taste can be found in the drawing of a table kept in the church of *SS. Annunziata* (M.I. Catalano, op. cit., Napoli, 1984, p. 395).

[48] A. D'Esposito, *Giovan Battista Cavagna, architetto romano a Napoli* dissertation on History of Architecture, Faculty of Literature and Philosophy, University of Naples, academical year 1985-86. Dr. Silvana Savarese kindly advised me to consult the document.

[49] These elements have to be considered as part of 1778 intervention (cnf. in the appendix, document n. 90). On that occasion, the marble-worker Antonio di Lucca was paid also for the restoration of the high altar, for the two holy-water fonts, that are at present near the door-way and for the doors nearby the little choirs.

[50] Cnf. document n. 90 in the Appendix.

[51] Even if Celano had already attributed the work to Fanzago (C. Celano, op. cit., p. 925) the information was published for the first time by Filangieri (R. Filangieri, op. cit., pp. 44-45, fig. XVI).

[52] G. Sigismondi, op. cit., p. 90.

[53] Cnf. documents n. 54, 55 in the Appendix; see also M. Pasculli Ferrara, E. Nappi, *Arte napoletana in Puglia dal XVI al XVIII secolo*, Fasano, 1983.

[54] According to an illusionistic effect of corresponding elements the whole is reproduced in a monochromatic fresco over the opposite wall, in the outer-sacristy.

[55] Cnf. the item by F. Nicolini, in *Dizionario Biografico degli Italiani*, Roma, 1960.

[56] *Documenti estratti...*, op. cit., 1940, pp. 457-458; cnf. also document n. 30 in the Appendix.

[57] At this regard it is interesting to observe that according to the documents (cnf. document n. 29 in the Appendix) Angelo Landi worked in the chapel in 1614 where he made a lavabo that might have been at the same place of the actual XVIII century one. So we may presume that the presence of Fanzago is due to Landi's intervention. The first was called again by the governors' of the *Monte* for some other marginal intervention.

[58] The popularity of these decorative motives is testified by two «stemmi» (coat of arms) found in the Cathedral of Salerno; they are surmounted by angels with open arms as those by Fanzago.

[59] Some recent studies have excluded from this phase of Fanzago's production the monument to Michele Gentile in the Cathedral of Barletta, attributed to the sculptor (cnf. M. PASCULLI FERRARA, E. NAPPI, *op. cit.*, pp. 157-161.

[60] A. SPINOSA, «Cosimo Fanzago, lombardo a Napoli» in *Prospettiva*, 1976, 7, pp. 10-26.

[61] The monument to the jurist Geronimo Flerio was attributed to Fanzago by Bologna (F. BOLOGNA, *Mostra del ritratto storico napoletano*, Catalogue of the art-exhibition, 1954, p. 24); the «putti» have been recently stolen.

[62] G. CANTONE, op. cit., p. 39.

[63] M.S. MORMONE, cit., Napoli 1984, p. 180.

[64] A. SPINOSA, «Precisazioni su Cosimo Fanzago», in *Antologia di Belle Arti*, 1984, 21-22, pp. 53-64.

[65] R. FILANGIERI, op. cit., p. 46.

[66] R. FILANGIERI, op. cit., p. 46.

[67] Cnf. documents n. 49, 50, in the Appendix.

[68] Cnf. documents n. 53, 54, 55, 56 in the Appendix and N. PASCULLI FERRARA, E. NAPPI, op. cit., p. 328.

[69] Cnf. documents n. 70, 82, 90 in the Appendix.

[70] T. FITTIPALDI, *Scultura napoletana del '700*, Napoli, 1980, p. 43.

[71] G. BORRELLI, *Il presepe Napoletano*, Napoli, 1970, p. 160. Recently, Elio Catello (E. CATELLO, «Francesco Solimena disegni e invenzioni per argentieri» in *Napoli Nobilissima*, XXIV, 1985, pp. 108-111) furtherly enriched the artist's biographic news by enlightening his relations with Solimena.

[72] A. BLUNT, *Neapolitan Baroque and Rococò Architecture*, London, 1975, fig. 227.

[73] Elio Catello kindly made me notice that an example which is very similar to that of the altars of the *Monte di Pietà*, realized in white marble, is the altar of *San Eustachio* in the crypt of the Cathedral of Acquaviva delle Fonti in Apulia. It is a Neapolitan work, with similar typology, with the sculptural groups by Matteo Bottigliero representing *S. Teofista* and the twins *Teofista* and *Agapito* at the two sides (1744). Cnf. M. PASCULLI FERRARA, E. NAPPI, op. cit., pp. 123-124.

[74] G. BORRELLI, op. cit., p. 171.

[75] Cnf. document n. 29 in the Appendix.

[76] Cnf. document n. 67 in the Appendix.

[77] M. MORELLI, L. CONFORTI, op. cit., p. 38.

[78] R. CAUSA, «Il manierismo e il Barocco», in *Sculture lignee in Campania*, catalogue of the art-exhibition, Napoli, 1950, p. 186.

[79] B. DE DOMINICI, *Vite dei Pittori, Scultori e Architetti Napoletani*, III, Napoli, 1742, p. 163.

[80] R. CAUSA, op. cit., p. 185.

[81] R. CAUSA, op. cit., p. 186.

[82] G. BORRELLI, op. cit., pp. 176-177.

[83] R. MIDDIONE, in *Il Patrimonio artistico del Banco di Napoli*, Napoli, 1984, pp. 46-51. It is indispensable to point out certain distinctions within the group of works published by Causa. It seems to me that in the sculptures of the *Gesù Nuovo*, of *SS. Filippo e Giacomo* and in the different types of guardian angels in the various Neapolitan churches, an Andalusian influence is manifested which is different from the wooden group of the *Monte di Pietà*. A more spiritual rather than phisical pathos is typical of the art of that area, where more familiar themes are delineated (M.E. GOMEZ MORENO, *La cultura spagnola*, Milano, 1968, p. 13). Andalusian sculptors never veered from their ideals of grace and idealized naturalistic visions, far from the Michelangelo-like Romanism that characterized the school in the North of Spain and from expressionistic exasperations. Some confrontations can be made with certain works, by F. Ocampo such as *Gesù Nazareno* of the church of *S. Bartolomeo a Carmona* (1607), or with works by the joung M. Montanes as *Cristo della Clemenza* of the Cathedral of Seville (1603), the *Cristo con la croce* of the confraternity of Silence in Seville (1611 c.a.) and some details of the retablo of *Sant'Isidoro del Campo* in Seville (1609). (Cnf. M. ELENA GOMEZ MORENO, «Escultura del siglo XVII», in *Ars Hispaniae*, Madrid, 1963, pp. 41, 136-137, 143.

[84] M.I. CATALANO, *Scultori Toscani a Napoli*, op. cit., pp. 124-125.

The Restoration of the Frescoes
by Annachiara Alabiso

Today as in no other historical period we lament the negligence surrounding our artistic patrimony, notwithstanding the delays and the lack of intervention that still exist.

As a matter of fact, it is impossible to be indifferent to the «death» of an artistic masterpiece, even if, in most cases, we are powerless to be of any help. It is right to affirm «non si deve restaurare a meno che non sia inevitabile»[1], i.e. we must make restorations only when necessary, while, on the contrary, maintenance and preventive measures must be carried out costantly. But when, for a long period, nothing has been done, we can only intervene by restoring. By this we mean action in order to stop the degradation of a work of art and, consequently, to give it an original appeerence by eliminating all traces of previous unsuccessful interventions.

The new restoration will employ reversible materials, easily removable by further intervention; even if some operations such as «la pulitura sono sempre irreversibili»[2] because they remove the action of time which, nonetheless, is part of the history of any object.

The real problem is that in Italy we lack an overall concept of the maintenance of artistic works even if something is changing in that today when we plan a restoration we also plan maintenance by establishing when it has to be done.

An example is the marble Arch of *Alfonso D'Aragona* in Naples, 38 m. high, which is being restored. It has been established that every three years a «sollevatore», i.e. a vehicle with a crane and a cage, will be hired in order to check the state of the marble and to adopt special measures if necessary. Maintenance has already been planned for the majolica cloister of *Santa Chiara* in Naples as well, though only the research preliminary to the restoration has been done to date. Neverthless, it will be a simpler operation as there is no need for scaffolding.

Also the restoration of the rooms of the ex-congregation of the *Banco* and of the annexed chapel of the *Monte di Pietà*, is coupled with a plan of maintenance: the restorer himself, assisted by the art historian, will verify the condition of the frescoes, stuccoes, wooden seats and marble pieces that decorate the building and will intervene where necessary.

This inspection will obviously follow the ascertainments concerning the structure of the building (static and ceiling revision) which will be executed by the technical office of the *Banco di Napoli*, with particular care for those parts on which rest frescoes or stuccoes.

Obviously, the actual work of restoration has followed that of static consolidation and restoration of the rooms where the artistic works are kept. The work has been executed by the Monica Martelli-Castaldi «Conservation» Co. and directed by the *Sovrintendenza ai Beni Artistici e Storici di Napoli* in continuous consultation with the technical office of the *Banco di Napoli*. For historians of art, inspectors of superintendence and directors of works, accustomed as we are to fight against lack of funds, it would be wonderful to work in such an atmosphere as that created around this work. Everyone has taken part in it: from technicians of the *Istituto Centrale per il Restauro* to restorers who frequently went beyond their line of duty.

As for the materials employed in the restoration of the *Monte di Pietà* building, the *Istituto Centrale per il Restauro* gave exhaustive advice and stratigraphs before and after the intervention.

Only experimented and tested products have been employed both because the artistic masterpieces were too important to risk experimenting with new products and because the intervention was not so complicated as to require the employment of chance novelties.

Some rooms have required a complete intervention of restoration: consolidation of the plaster, fixing of the painted surface, cleaning, filling of «lacunae» and pictorial integration. Other rooms have required mere cleaning operations.

Everything has been accompanied by detailed written and photographic reports. It is essential for an intervention of restoration not only to be dated but also well-documented by reports and photographs in order to avoid a repetition of what has happened all too often in the past. In these cases, lacking any reference of material, it was necessary to rely on mere hypotheses. The history of the *Monte di Pietà* too lacks of any reference to past operations. Only by careful and prolonged observation of the artistic works, of stratifications and stylistic characteristics has it been deduced that the frescoes and the stucco-works have been restored twice in the past.

The first restoration took place at the end of the XVIII century, after 31 July 1786, when a fire devastated the whole building[3], and the second one in the first years of this century, after 3 June 1903, when a second fire damaged the building[4].

A marble inscription in the entrance-hall of the building informs us that several works were done in 1904. They must have continued until 1907 and they concerned the re-construction of some walls and a new destination to be given to the rooms of the ex-congregation of the *Banco*[5]. On that occasion, the painter Paolo Vetri[6] restored the frescoes on the front of the Chapel and a certain Fatiguso restored the stucco-works[7].

Already in 1902 the restorers Agostino Conte and Pasquale Chiariello restored the painting on canvas for the left altar of the Chapel, the *Resurrezione* commissioned to Ippolito Borghese, passed to Gerolamo Imparato and, at his death, executed by Fabrizio Santafede in 1608[8].

A general restoration of the building, and particularly of the artistic works that decorate it, was anticipated in the book about the Chapel of the *Monte di Pietà* by Mario Morelli and Luigi Conforti in 1899[9].

In the introduction, the publisher Gennaro Priore affirms that at the end of the previous year (1898), Nicola Miraglia, general manager of the *Banco*, had asked for a report on the conditions of the Chapel.

In Priore's words, the general manager «preoccupato del deplorevole stato di abbandono in cui trovasi la cappella... richiamava l'attenzione di Guido Baccelli Ministro della Pubblica Istruzione... Fu dal prefato Ministro dato incarico alla Direzione del Museo Nazionale di Napoli di esaminare e riferire intorno all'importanza artistica e allo stato della Cappella del Pio Monte. E il Commendatore Giulio de Petra a ciò delegava l'Ispettore Mario Morelli, il quale senza indugio compilò una minuziosa ed elaborata relazione, che venne trasmessa al Ministro e al Direttore Generale del Banco di Napoli. Con la medesima relazione si concludeva per la necessità di un accurato e coscienzioso studio di ricerca sulla provenienza degli oggetti d'arte esistenti nella Cappella del Monte, onde ottenere una più precisa identificazione ed una più esatta valutazione».

The XVIII century restoration had consisted of nailing the detached pieces of plaster with L-shaped metallic clamps, filling in the spaces where colour had fallen by stuccoing with a lime and sand mortar and restoring «a falso» with oil-colours.

The restoration executed at the beginning of this century employed the same technique with regard to the plaster. In fact, four-sided handmade nails were employed, probably pressure shot into the gypsum, to serve as a hook for a lacing with metallic thread intended to brace the fissures.

These superimposed restorations were seen to be ruinous. The second intervention consisted in removing all the metal clamps from the preceding works and stuccoing the resulting holes with plaster at the same time making an infinite quantity of new holes for the new nails.

This last intervention was also responsible for repairing small holes and fissures with plaster, the larger ones with water soluble neutral colours.

The present restoration began in the last months of 1983 starting with the frescoes by Belisario Corenzio in the rooms on the upper floor of the building of the *Monte di Pietà*, once headquarters of the congregation of the *Banco* and now housing offices: the so-called rooms of *Silenzio*, *Pazienza* and *Concordia*. The restoration commenced with these rooms both because the frescoes here were in the worst conditions and because it presented the opportunity to test a procedure to adopt later in the Chapel, whose frescoes are by Belisario Corenzio and followers as well, among whom Luigi Rodriguez.

The first room is named *Silenzio* because of the bearded figure depicted in the centre of the vault with a crown of laurel on his head, a large grey garment falling to his ankles and his forefinger to his lips in a gesture invoking silence. A grey and clouded sky creates the background. The painting, edged by a contemporary stucco frame, is accompanied by an inscription in a volute «Eximia est virtus praestare silentia rebus».

To find an example in Naples which inspired this painting we must go back to 1544-45, when Vasari painted a similar figure among the allegories in the vault of the ex-refectory of the church of *Monteoliveto*. But since Vasari's figure also has the characteristic attribute of a horse's bit, it has been interpreted as *Obbedienza* rather than *Silenzio*[10].

Our *Silenzio* was executed in tempera on sand and lime plaster, a somewhat crumbly and thin surface which has not weathered the ravages of time. The paint layer was extremely weak and powdery, there were several detachments at the various levels of the preparatory layers of rendering and both the stucco-frame and the surface of the painting had been heavily repainted during previous restorations. In addition to this, there were numerous «lacunae» and an abundance of nails. Corenzio had laid on the plaster a very light grey base, probably in order to make the tonalities of the mortar more uniform and to prevent it from absorbing too much colour.

Several incisions were noted whereas there is no trace of a preparatory drawing with the exception of the letters on the frieze, made with a technique called «spolvero» (tecnique employed to transfer a drawing with the same proportions onto a wall or onto wood or canvas as well. It consists in passing chalk or charcoal, in this case charcoal, over the pierced contours of the drawing so that an exact trace remains on the surface below). In the *Silenzio* the colours have been spread with light brush strokes in depicting the clothes and heavier strokes on the upper part of the drapery, the shoulders, the head, the hands and the feet.

The effect of a lawn where various types of plants and grasses are drawn with great care, is achieved by superimposing light and dark green, warm and cold tonalities, with leaves and blades of grass only slightly accentuated.

As often occurs in wall paintings, the most poorly preserved part was the sky — completely abrased, almost irrecognizable — with vague hints of clouds depicted with clear, full brush strokes and veiled in trasparent layers of pale blue and pink to give the desired nuances.

The condition of the sky leads us to suppose that there had been a heavy infiltration of water from the upper floor, confirmed by the presence of visible white saline efflorescences. The surface was covered by a layer of dirt as well as by numerous over paintings. Moreover, the entire painted surface had been fixed with a layer of animal glue which, not having been completely absorbed in several places, was clearly visible in oblique light.

There were also three «lacunae», the largest one high on the right of the observer, a smaller one low on the left and another one at the bottom of the gown. Many distinct fissures ran transversally over the painting and some small ones of various sizes and shapes covered the whole surface, particularly near the head.

The present day intervention consisted in fixing the colour on the wall painting by the use of an acrylic emulsion dissolved in a water solution. The subsequent operation consisted in the consolidation of the losses of adhesion between the plaster and the wall by means of injections of «a vinyl emulsion» dissolved in water.

Successively the saline efflorescences were eliminated by applying compresses soaked in distilled water until complete drying.

The nails and metal threads were eliminated too. Steps were not taken to remove all the nails because some of them had penetrated quite deeply and removing them would have meant damaging the surrounding area of colour, provoking a new detachment of the plaster. Since there was no great distance between the nails, the entire surface would have come away.

The most difficult operation resulted to be the cleaning. It was carried out by eliminating the fixative used in previous interventions applying small compresses soaked in an organic solvent, removing the retouchings and repaintings soluble in water, eliminating the greasy dirt oil repaintings with compresses of cellulose pulp soaked with a mixture of slightly basic salts. Organic solvents were used to remove the more stubborn layers of repainting. The next step was the removal of the neutral plaster stuccoing and almost all the stucco fillings in the nail holes.

All the big repainting «a falso» — executed on stuccoing made of lime and sand mortar — were left intact. The large areas of missing plaster were stuccoed below the surface while other areas were restored at surface level with a mortar of lime and fine river sand.

Having concluded the operations of conservation, the next consideration was the aesthetical appearence of the work. After cleaning, the surface appeared very abrased, with extensive loss of colour and innumerable holes and fissures to be closed. All the surface weave of the patina was re-established by a light water colour glazing; «tratteggio» with water colours was used to cover the small missing portions which had been stuccoed.

A uniform glazing tone was executed over the areas where large portions of the painted surface had fallen. The central part of the allegorical figure's robe was left «a falso».

The last operation was the final fixing, executed with an acrylic resin laid on by brush strokes. It has a protective function, because it strengthens the painted surface and allows longer life to the restoration. The material used is *Paraloid* B72, already experimented for years and having the great advantage of reversibility i.e. it can be easily removed in a future intervention and furthermore it is inalterable in that it does not turn yellow, thus permitting a faithful interpretation of the work of art.

The second room in which the restoration has been done is decorated in the centre with the allegory *Pazienza*[11], a female figure in peasant dress standing in a meadow and carrying on her shoulders a farm tool which is no longer recognizable owing to numerous small areas of missing colour and to a large area of fallen plaster.

In the other two partitions, separated from the central scene by stucco frames (present in all the rooms) there are two pairs of «putti» (little angels) — one pair above, holding a representation of the *Monte di Pietà*, the other below, carrying a frieze with the word «Libenter».

All the paintings were executed in tempera on plaster of lime and sand. There too, can be seen the tones of the preparatory base but there are no traces of incisions. In comparison with the previous room, the colour here is much more consistent, the brush strokes more apparent in their clear tonalities and transparent glazing. The surface of the painting was entirely covered by a thick layer of dark yellow dirt and by numerous repaintings under which the colour, in many areas, is non-existent — in particular the entire sky, the field, the woman's face and the four «putti».

A large fissure, stuccoed and repaired «a falso» during the intervention at the beginning of this century, ran vertically over the central figure, widening in the lower part. A large neutral plaster stuccoing below the woman's face completely hid a missing arm, and part of another. On the «putti» in the upper scene, another stucco repair — belonging to the same intervention — ran diagonally from the left corner towards the lower part of the painting; a smaller repair was seen on the leg of the «putto» on the right. As for the «putti» in the lower scene, the entire right corner was found to be well reconstructed «a falso».

All the rest of the scene had been heavily repainted since there was practically none of the original colour remaining. In fact, the absence of colour was diffused especially on the right side where there was a greater presence of fissures as well, both on the «putti» and in the central scene.

In this room too, one sees evidence of the two different restorations with their resulting stuccoed holes, nails, metallic wires, repaintings.

Here too, there must have been problems of infiltration of water, evidenced by the formation of saline efflorescences, especially on the upper part of the central figure and in the two scenes with «putti».

The methods and materials used in this intervention are the same as in the *Silenzio* room though the greater depreciation has required a much more thorough and careful intervention, particularly during the colour fixing and reintegration phases where effort was made to salvage what was still visible of the original drawing and colours just darkening the missing areas with a water colour glazing, not repainting them.

The last room on the top floor requiring restorations was the *Concordia*[12] so-called because this virtue is represented in the centre of the vault, surrounded by the same stucco frame seen in the other rooms. It is a female figure wearing a crown of laurel and holding a glass chalice in one hand, a scepter in the other; one foot is shifted slightly to the rear and beneath it lies a bundle of rods surrounded by leaves and blades of grass. Above her, two «putti» with fluttering draperies hold the symbol of the *Monte di Pietà*. Below the painting there is an inscription in a volute surmounted by a shell which reads «Concordia parvae res crescunt».

This allegory is also present in the church of *Monte Oliveto*, again painted by Vasari, but here he represented *Concordia* with some weapons on the ground, with a bundle of rods in her hands and some other broken rods at her feet. The surface of the painting was covered by a thick layer of dirt and some fragments had come away.

A fissure more than a centimeter deep ran vertically across the painting from top to bottom. In the restoration carried out in the first part of the 20th century the *Concordia* had been stuccoed with plaster and retouched with oil colours that actually overshot the original edges. The same technique was employed in certain less extensive missing parts. The sky had been completely repainted with darker colours, water soluble, which, once removed, left visible, extensive abrasions of the paint layer. The detached areas of plaster were held up by nails and metallic wires.

Compared with the paintings previously described, this one was certainly in better conditions. Therefore, although the methodology and materials employed have been the same, this restoration was less complicated and took far less time. Once the restoration of the upper floor was completed, work was begun on the ground floor which, too, was once part of the congregation of the «Banco» and today is used as auction room and for the sale of unredeemed pledges.

In the first restored room, in addition to the central painting, the lunettes of the vault are decorated as well. The original painting of the central part — like all the decoration — must date back to 1601[13] but it has been completely lost and was replaced by «a fresco» by Paolo Vetri representing *Sapienza* — a seated female figure with a book in one hand and a candlestick in the other. A contemporary inscription in a volute reads «Omnia comspicio».

The side lunettes of the vault, dating back to the 17th century, represent figures of angels, decorative motifs and monochrome scenes. The reinforcement of the wall paintings was carried out by Pasquale Chiariello in 1907[14].

The central scene is done in fresco and three «giornate» (a day's work) are easily visible. Traces of indirect incisions are noted on the mantle of the female figure as well as direct incisions on the architectonic motifs. There are, however, no traces of preliminary drawings. The work presented a large missing portion, circular, in the lower area. The plaster was detached at the surface in several spots, with several long, thin fissures, but the general condition of the painted surface was good. The remaining paintings in the side lunettes are done «a secco» — i.e. on a dry surface of lime and sand mortar covered with a white layer of lime — and they were in extremely bad condition. The surface layer of plaster came away at the touch of a finger since it was no longer adherent to the underlying layer («arriccio»), which was crumbly and weakened. The painted surface was fragile and flaky. The previous intervention had included an attempt to support the detached plaster by «sewing» the fissures with nails and metallic thread. The filling of losses had been executed in plaster and the countless «lacunae» and abrasions had been completely repainted with no respect for the border and with colours soluble in water or in organic solvents.

Fixing of the paint layer had not been necessary in the well-preserved central scene but in the rest of the vault the pigment layer had been fixed by repeated applications of dissolved acrylic resin or, where the colour had flaked off, by injecting the resin drop by drop in order to make the flakings adhere again. Injections of polyvinil acetate in emulsion were used for the small detachments of the rendering, while the large detached areas were injected with lime and pozzuolana, shoring the area during the operation. Here, too, not all the nails were removed because many were deeply embedded and any attempts to extract them would have endangered the surrounding area, considering the close proximity of the many nails.

Cleaning operations began with the removal of the repainted areas done in water-soluble colours, eliminating the dirt by employing water or acetone for the more tenacious surfaces. Moreover, all the plaster work which had been applied in previous interventions was removed, most of which was actually on top of the original painted surface. Mortar of lime and river sand was then used for the new applications of plaster, working below the surface on the larger, illegible areas and at surface level on the less seriously damaged spots. Water colour glazing and small corrections with pastel crayons were necessary to integrate the areas where the paint layer was missing — a customary procedure following major interventions of this type.

In the room called *Fecondità* the vault is composed of three panels. The central scene, restored in 1907 by Paolo Vetri [15], represents the main theme with a standing female figure, one hand on her hip and the other hand holding a dish full of fruit. A dolphin lies at her feet, its tail rolled. The smaller side panels display pairs of «puttini», above and below the central figure. The «putti» in the lower scene hold an inscription reading «Fructum affert». The central part of the upper scene is completely lost and was restuccoed and repainted in a previous intervention. During cleaning operations — once removed the repainting that covered part of the original — an examination of the remaining fragments revealed the erroneus interpretation made by the restorer, who had placed an inscription between the «puttini» whereas originally there had probably been a pillow, or drapery. The painting was done «a secco», i.e. on dry plaster composed of lime and sand, the colours applied with brush strokes on a neutral light grey surface. A large fissure ran vertically across the central panel. Further long fissures were seen on the side panels and the precarious static condition of the paintings was again demonstrated by the presence of nails and metallic threads. The methods and materials were the same employed in the preceding room and in the following one, where the central figure in the ceiling is *La Terra*, a female figure crowned with laurel and holding a sheath of corn in one hand, a hoop in the other. She is standing in a field of leaves and grass. Two fluttering angels carry a flowing fascia and below them is the inscription «Condita conservare meum est» in a volute decorated with shells, angel heads and the habitual symbol of the *Monte di Pietà*.

This painting, too, was done «a secco» on lime and sand plaster. Some indirect incisions can be seen on the ears of corn while direct incising is revealed along the monochrome fasciae framing the painting. Much damage has been caused by an infiltration of moisture from the upper floor. In various places the plaster is detached and the painted surface is lost in many areas, especially in the lower left part where saline efflorescences are evident. During the restoration at the beginning of the 20th century the missing portions had been filled with gypsum and animal glue plaster, overlapping the original surface and using repainting colours which were found difficult to remove.

The last phase of the restoration concerns the complex of the chapel of the *Monte di Pietà*, formed by the church and four smaller rooms: a little sacristy and the oratory on one side, the room of the Congregation of the Bank with its entrance hall on the other. All these rooms were decorated with stuccoes and wall paintings by Belisario Corenzio together with important apprentices from his workshop, among whom Luigi Rodriguez. These 17th century frescoes integrate splendidly with the frescoes and decorations done in the fourth decade of the 18th century by certain apprentices of Giuseppe Bonito — and are similar to other paintings being restored today in the various Archive rooms of the *Banco di Napoli* in *Tribunali* street.

Restoration began in the vault of the church which is divided into three bays, the central bay being slightly larger than the other two. The decoration consists of eleven main scenes — separated from one another by variously shaped gilded frames — portraying the *Passion of Christ*. In addition, there are forty-seven smaller panels with decorative motifs, «putti» and symbols of the Passion.

The stucco work framing the frescoes is characterized by a number of decorative elements: garlands, shields, heads of winged «putti», crests with the symbol of the *Monte di Pietà*, rosettes, etc.

This stucco work was executed first, leaving the panels empty and in readiness for the painted scenes.

A layer of coarse plaster («arriccio») was laid onto the wall destined for the stucco decorations and for the paintings. After having delimitated the spaces with the help of a plumb-line and incising the edges in the still-wet plaster, frames and mouldings were realized with special patterns on an initial layer of coarse lime mortar. The patterns were moved along parallel guidelines fixed to the surface in order to obtain the relief shape of the frame, the surface was then covered with a final, white layer, smoothed and finished by hand. The decorative elements such as thumb-printing, notching and vegetation motifs were executed «a stampo», i.e. directly onto the mortar and probably by using a wooden mould. The higher reliefs such as capitals, heads of «putti», shields and garlands had an internal reinforcement made of nails and iron wire. The reinforcement was covered with a mixture of lime mortar and pozzuolana on which the reliefs were sketched. Successively the final layer of white mortar was applied and the detailed forms and motifs were completed. The stucco work was then gilded where decided.

Minor detached areas were present almost everywhere between the first preparatory layer on the wall and the final white surface layer, especially in the areas where the reliefs were more projected. Most of the small decorations which had been directly applied to the final layer were detached from the «arriccio» and in hazardous conditions.

The problem more clearly concerned the bas-reliefs rather than the high-relief stuccoes, where adhesion was quite good. Only in some places the stuccoes presented signs of cracking, probably due to their more fragile surface. Numerous stretches of decorative elements were lost as well as lengthy pieces of the framework which had been replaced during previous restorations by false, rather gross reconstructions characterized by only slightly accentuated modelling or, even more surprising, painted with a trompe-l'oeil technique. The stucco work, too, has supposedly undergone two interventions similar to the ones concerning the other decorations of the building, the first: after 1786, which fixed the gilding, stuccoed lesions, repainted the white background and reconstructed, «ex novo», the arches on the altars. The second intervention occurred at the beginning of this century, after the deterioration of the gilding, which was completely repainted. In addition to this, the crumbling reliefs were reconstructed and another coat of white was applied to the background — this time with water-soluble material. We can also presume that at this time, too, iron nails and metallic wires were secured and the lesions repaired. The last restoration revealed the loss of the forehead of one of the four central «putti», parts of their wings and parts of the capitals. Probably the loss was due to oxidation which had taken place in the supporting iron nails.

During one of the two preceding interventions (probably after 1786) a shellac fixative was applied to the gilding, damaging it irreparably. In fact, the gold-leaf reacted by curling up instead of forming the usual scale-like surface which can easily be fixed by an adhesive. The knotted appearance caused by the shellac could not be softened nor smoothed out along the surface.

Fortunately the undamaged gilded parts (30-40% of the surface) are well preserved. The most significant losses concern the smooth parts of the frames, the hair and wings of the angels and the four capitals. Small stucco repairs were seen everywhere, but fortunately the underlying gilded part is well preserved. In an attempt to recover the original intact quality of the work, the restorer who intervened at the beginning of this century uniformly painted, in dark ochre, all the gilded parts (the gilt must have appeared quite dark to

Chapel, detail of one the winged «putti» decorating the vault.
Note the crackings and losses of the stucco-work due to the oxidation of internal nails

Chapel, decorative elements of the stucco-work in the vault

him, due to the darkering of the shellac). He then took care to lighten the effect by touching up with light ochre in the areas in high-relief and where the light falls. Furthermore, he actually sprayed the work with white in an effort to imitate the original areas where the fallen gilding had left tiny white spots. The white backgrounds have also been repainted twice, one darker, unsoluble layer in the first restoration and a second, lighter one, more easily soluble in water. The false parts on the underside of the arches were repainted, together with the remaining gilded parts, with highly resistant colours able to withstand any kind of cleaning process.

The present-day restoration has attempted to bring the original to light in the best possible manner by firstly eliminating the thick layer of dust and grease caused by candle smoke and atmospheric conditions. It was decided to remove the repaintings covering the gilded areas and the white backgrounds; some false stuccoing has been left, delimitating their outlines exactly so as to distinguish them from the original at the moment of reintegration. As for the gold leafing, efforts were made to retrieve certain parts by impregnation with fixatives and successive pressing with a spatula. This method proved successful only in the few cases where the leafing had become raised; the curled up portions were irretrievable. All the work was carried out in a very articulated fashion. Various materials were employed with respect to the type of detachment and the area to be treated. In-depth detachments were treated with injections of hydraulic mortar of lime and pozzuolana. Acrylic resins in a watery emulsion were used to treat surface detachments. Fissures were filled with pozzuolana and lime augmented by pumice for the top layers.

Plaster, canary seed and water were used to attach the decorations which had come away or fallen and in some cases it was necessary to employ the addition of an adhesive. Cleaning operations on the areas with gold leaf were carried out with soft brushes and water, following a protective or preventive fixing. They were then refinished using scalpels for the removal of excess stuccoing or layers of stubborn paint.

The white areas were cleaned using bristle brushes with water. The vast areas covered with stubborn repainting were refinished mechanically. The most recent stuccoing (which had replaced the ones made in earlier restorations but were to be eliminated as unacceptable from an aesthetic point of view) was executed with plaster and canary seed — for the minor repair jobs — and with a mortar of lime and fine marble dust for the larger ones.

In the areas where the missing parts were more consistent, a first layer of lime mortar, pozzuolana and sand was laid on followed by a layer of lime and marble dust, remaining faithful to the original techniques which have served as a guide in the entire modern-day restoration. The missing parts were reconstructed by free-hand modelling. As for the decorations done «a stampo», steps were taken to construct a cast and pour the final plaster. Both the stuccoes and the frescoes were retouched simultaneously. The stuccoes were treated with water colours in subsequent glazing to attenuate the tonality of the parts lacking gold leaf. The missing parts which had been stuccoed were reintegrated with studied moderation so as not to disturb the intactness of the whole from a colour point of view but, at the same time, to render them recognizable at close quarters.

Here, too, the painted surface was intersected by two long lesions running along the vault and crossing at the centre. During the 18th century restoration the central part of some of the scenes had been reconstructed «a falso» in «fresco» technique, i.e. not only had the personages been repainted but also the mortar had been contrived again with lime and rather coarse sand. Owing to further movements of the structure, the lesions repaired in the first restoration came open again and were successively filled with a smoother, harder mortar on which repainting was executed «a secco» — superimposed on the original 17th century ones as well as on the frescoes of the late 18th century. Naturally, these repaintings had dulled the original and had, in some places, created a proper falsification. In the *Lavanda dei piedi* a completely invented character appeared in the centre of the scene; in the *Ultima cena* a handsome still-life of two copper and pewter pots had been covered by a coarsely-shaped cylindrical container; in the *Trasfigurazione* thick foliage had been painted over the first character top left and, in this scene, the hair and beards had been ridiculously thickened; even the marbled pilaster strips in the counter-façade had been falsified.

The detached parts near the lesions were extensive and seriously damaged; due to problems of statics, in some places the plaster had swelled.

The painted surface was in quite good condition. Only in the scene of the *Flagellazione* had the colour become scaly. All the frescoed parts were in a good state while the «a secco» or dry decorations had, for the most part, dropped off owing to their more delicate nature. The painted surface was dulled by a uniform layer of dust (even smog), grease (candle smoke) and fixative.

A heavy saline efflorescence was visible only on the figure of *San Gerolamo*, at the right of the high altar, and has been eliminated like the efflorescences found in the Congregation room — with woodpulp compresses of distilled water until complete drying. By means of a close inspection it has been possible to analyze the techniques used in the pictorial decoration. On the wall of the counter-façade — near the most significant missing portions — the fall of plaster had revealed the existence of a single, uniform layer of «arriccio» along the entire surface, underneath the painted and stuccoed decoration, composed of lime mortar, sand and pozzuolana, on which is superimposed the rendering — made of lime, sand and pozzuolana as well. Owing to the reduced dimensions of the panels, but also to the technical skill of Corenzio and his fellow workers, the marks of the «giornate» are no easily visible (they can, however, be seen clearly in *Cristo presentato al popolo* and in *Cristo coronato di spine*). Traces of the tools used to apply and flatten the plaster are easily seen. It has been smoothed on with great care and, in oblique light, the surface appears quite granulous.

Whereas in the rooms of the Congregation only direct and indirect incising was observed (in the chapel vault, respectively for architectonic aspects and for figures) here some traces of pouncing (perforated patterns) can be seen in the decorations painted «a secco» and in quick preparatory drawings in black, ochre and red in the decorative fascias. The colour is laid on «a fresco» with a thick, rich paste, or it is glazed on. Shading is achieved with thick, clear strokes or, utilizing the clear background colour, by proceeding with repeated

Chapel, counter-façade *Trasfigurazione*. Detail showing one of the deep structural lesions of the walls

 Coarse mortar painted in «fresco»

Fine mortar painted in «secco»

Overpaintings in «secco»

Cement fillings nails and metal wires

Detail in the following page

Chapel, counter façade *Trasfigurazione*. Graphic of the two previous restorations

Chapel, counter façade *Trasfigurazione*. Details of the left and right groups during the cleaning showing the two previous restorations, a cleaning test and the nails and metal wires

Chapel, counter-façade *Trasfigurazione*. The «lacuna» of the lesion after the application of the new plaster

Chapel, *Flagellazione*. Detail of the head of Christ before the intervention

Chapel, *Flagellazione*. Detail during the integration of the lesion in «tratteggio» thecnique

Chapel, *Flagellazione*. After restoration.

Chapel, *San Gerolamo*. Detail before restoration showing the salin efflorescences covering the surface and the nail used to contain the plaster

Chapel, *San Gerolamo*, After the restoration

transparent strokes. A particular technique is used to obtain the effect of volume and shadow. Small lines or brush strokes in tones of ochre or brown are calculated according to the direction of the natural light.

This same technique has been observed in the *Storie di San Gennaro*, by Domenichino, in the Cathedral of Naples, now under restoration. The diagonal decorative strips in the cross vault and the triangles painted on green backgrounds above the four scenes surmounting the balconies were painted « a secco » with preparatory drawing in « spolvero » technique.

The present intervention was begun with a protective procedure — fixing of the flaking off paint layer and applying them again to the plaster by means of small injections of acrylic resins in emulsion. Fixing of the powdery paint layer of the « a secco » work was achieved by spraying with acrylic resins in solution; a protective facing of the swollen areas of plaster was carried out using Japanese paper and watery solutions of carboxyl methyl cellulose. Following this preliminary phase, reinforcement of the plaster was achieved by injections of hydraulic mortar. The lesions discovered after the removal of the stuccoing from the previous restoration were plugged with fragments of bricks and, wherever, possible, injected with hydraulic mortar. On the surface they were refinished with successive stuccoing of hydraulic mortar in a paste. Except for the cases where the nails of the previous interventions had penetrated in depth and their removal might have caused further damage to the surrounding surfaces, the nails were eliminated together with all the copper wires used to hold them. The mortar painted « a fresco » in the earlier intervention was preserved with the exception of the edges of the lacunae. The mortar applied in the 20th century intervention (save those in good condition) and the thin cement stuccoes possibly executed during the sixties were removed, the former because they were detached and the latter because their chemical composition was inadequate.

Cleaning operations were carried out in two distinct phases: firstly, woodpulp compresses soaked with a mixture of slightly basic salts were used, but despite this intervention the surface appeared dull owing to the persistence of a thin and diffuse grey film.

Steps were then taken to apply compresses with a saturate solution of ammonium carbonate. On completion of this operation the missing portions were stuccoed with lime mortar and river sand.

With an eye to balancing the whole aspect and reaching a solution as similar as possible to the original state, the painted surfaces were glazed with water colours where the patina had disappeared. Moreover, efforts were made to reduce the effect caused by abrasions, by the loss of colour and by the small stuccoing jobs performed in the past.

The following intervention took place in the entrance hall and in the room of the Congregation of the *Monte di Pietà*, almost completely painted during the first half of the 18th century with decorations composed of volutes, masks, rosettes, shells, allegorical figures of the four seasons and the portraits of Carlo di Borbone and his wife Maria Amalia di Sassonia. The only surviving 17th century painting is the *Soccorso*, attributed to Belisario Corenzio, depicted on the ceiling of the room, in a contemporary frame that was gilded in the 18th century. It is a winged figure, breast bared, the right hand raised on high and the left hand clenching a bag of money. An inscription immediately over the frame — reworked by Paolo Vetri in 1907 reads, «Si bene quid facias, facies cito»[16].

All the central part was repainted on smooth plaster in the 20th century intervention. Small missing portions were noted on the remaining parts of the original painting, stuccoed with the same type of mortar used in the reconstruction. The «lacunae» had been caused by the removal of nails used in the 18th century intervention in an attempt to solve problems of detachment of the plaster. The inscription and the lateral panels were repainted at this time. All the decorative motifs which had been covered with a protective varnish showed traces of the same type of intervention seen on the 17th century painting. Retouching on the fillings and missing portions of the painted surface were executed with water-colours. The lower part of the walls was repainted «a fresco», leaving intact the portraits of the king and queen. Reconstructed mortar, preceding the «a fresco» intervention, was found on the wall to the right of the portrait of Maria Amalia. More recent retouchings can be observed when comparing the wall today with a photograph taken in the 60's showing the damage caused by humidity and saline efflorescences. Curiously enough, in the scene on the vault depicting a figure holding a crescent, another sketchy drawing can be made out through the painted surface which has nothing to do with the present decorations. Generally speaking, the colours have been laid on with great skill. Certain details, and the shading (in the portraits, for example) were achieved with rich mixtures of colour. All the panels, rosettes and volutes had been embellished with subtle gold shading, almost completely lost today.

In this room the most afflicted areas were the painted bases of the walls. Extensive portions of colour were missing and, in the less serious instances, the painted part was covered with saline efflorescences caused by capillary humidity — which also gave rise to the loose condition of the plaster and to a widespread detachment of the «arriccio» coat. The problem was less serious in regard to the vault and, in the central portion, it was confined to the edges of the fissures and the juncture between the reconstructed mortar and the original one. The painted surface is also in better condition on the vault. The present day restoration includes the conservation of all the reconstructed «a fresco» and «a secco» areas. Saline efflorescences were eliminated by repeated «washings»; portions of detached plaster were reinforced by injections of hydraulic mortar and the lesions stuccoed with lime mortar and sand. Fixing of the detached or faded areas executed with Japanese paper saturated with emulsified acrylic resin. Dirt and old retouching jobs were removed with cold water and a sponge, followed by glazing with water soluble crayons or watercolours. The more seriously damaged walls were restored on the lower areas by glazing.

The final restoration concerned the sacristy, a room decorated with monochrome grey allegorical scenes on the vault, the walls, windows and doors, i.e. *Carità*, *Pietà*, *Sapienza Divina*, standing on pedestals of trompe-l'oeil gilt. The gilded backgrounds are trompe-l'oeil lattices through which the blue sky can be seen. Lining the walls are valuable walnut wardrobes and stalls embellished with gilt carving and gilded bronze decorations. All the wall

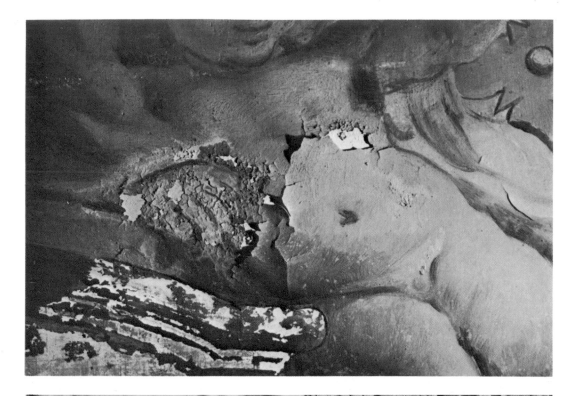

Sacristy, detail showing the flaking of the pain layers before and after the treatment

Sacristy, same area after consolidation and fixing of the paint layer and integration of worn golden areas using water colours

decoration was probably done by Giuseppe Bonito who, in 1742[17], executed the *Carità*, painted on canvas, which adorns the centre of the vault[18].

The tufa wall was first treated with a layer of plaster of lime, sand and pozzuolana followed by a thinner layer of lime and marble dust. The final layer was composed of an extremely fine mixture of gypsum and animal glue. The colour (originally blue, as seen by microscopic examination) had assumed a greenish tone due to oxidation of the varnish originally covering it. The gilt decorations were made on this surface, followed by the «a secco» painting of the «putti» and allegorical figures. A stratigraph reveals the presence — under the gilt— of a thin, opaque layer tinted with yellow earth which may be the «missione» indicating the drawing to be gilded. The frames and capitals were gilded over a red clay preparation and the drawings for the decorations were executed by pouncing.

Movement due to static pressure has caused structural damages to this room as well; lesions beginning in the centre of the vault, continuing along the walls and in the splayed windows were «sewn» with copper alloy clamps. The fillings of «lacunae» overlapped the original surface, but the gilt work and colours were in perfect harmony with the 18th century original decor. An opaque effect was observed on the gilded parts in as the fixative had turned slightly reddish and time-worn. The lower parts and some of the figures had been entirely repainted during the 20th century intervention, but only an extremely careful examination at close quarters permitted distinguishing the false from the original. The most serious problems of preservation were disclosed in oblique light, where detached parts were seen of the thin, preparatory layer and of the gold leafing. Fortunately, there were only a few detached areas between the wall and the plaster. The preparatory layer was generally disassociated from its base, more markedly in the lower parts, in the decorations in relief and, above all, in the reworked areas.

The operations perfomed in the present day intervention included fixing the gold leaf detachments with injections of an acrylic resin in a water emulsion; fixing the scaly surfaces of the painting with the same preparation; consolidating the missing portions with hydraulic mortar of lime and brick powder. Several applications were made of a further acrylic resin dissolved in organic solvent to remedy the disassociation of the preparatory layer. Cleaning was carried out using compresses of a saturate ammonium carbonate solution whereas the repaintings and false areas were refinished with a thinner. Glazing with water-colours was executed on all the areas where the gold had deteriorated. The most significant missing parts were stuccoed with lime mortar and marble dust and reintegrated in «tratteggio» technique with water-colours. A thin film of Paraloid B 72 — an acrylic varnish — was spread over the entire surface, its purpose being protective as well as aesthetic.

Restoration operations will be completed with the cleaning of the marble statues on the façade of the *Monte di Pietà* Chapel, and, even more significant, the restoration of the monochrome frescoes on the front which today are barely visible.

Their restoration is even more remarkable when we consider that this is the only painted façade that has been restored in Naples. Moreover, it is the only edifice in Naples boasting of works ascribed to such important artists as

Battistello Caracciolo (the six «puttini»), Luigi Rodriguez (the figures of *Fede* and *Speranza*) and Alessandro Hernandez (author of the panels)[19].

Thus we are taking steps to conclude one of the most momentous operations ever achieved in Naples in these last years, the restoration of a 17th-18th century bulding that even today carries out the purpose for which it was conceived.

We can only express our wish that here is the first step on the road to a rebirth of the greatest and most discredited historical centre in the world everything has been denied to it, except its undeniable beauty.

[1] I.F.L.A., *Conservazione e restauro nelle biblioteche*, in «Le biblioteche. Quaderni di Lavoro», Firenze 1982, n. 3, p. 6.

[2] H. JEDRZEJEWSKA, *Principi di restauro*, Firenze, 1983, p. 12.

[3] R. FILANGIERI DI CANDIDA, *I banchi di Napoli dalle origini alla costituzione del banco delle due Sicilie*, 1539-1808, Napoli, 1940, I, p. 137. Restoration took place in 1798. Cnf. the documents nn. 98-99-100 edited by E. Nappi in this volume, where Giovanni d'Errico, Nicola Manco and the well-known Angelo Mozzillo are mentioned. The first, «indoratore» is mentioned for the clearning and reconstruction of the gilding «così nella volta di nostra chiesa che delle sue mura»; the second, «stuccatore» is mentioned «per diversi accomodi di sua arte fatti nelle mura e nella volta di nostra chiesa» and finally, Angelo Mozzillo, «pittore» is mentioned for the retouching of some figures «esistenti nelle mura e lamia di nostra chiesa».
We have no information about Giovanni D'Errico and Nicola Manco, while we know something about Angelo Mozzillo from 1777 to 1805. He had Neapolitan origins and was famous as Giuseppe Bonito's apprentice thanks to his activity in the internal area nearby the *Vesuvio*. At this regard, we have to remember the fresco *Madonna e Santi Francescani* in *San Lorenzo* in *Ottaviano* (signed and dated 1777), the frescoes *Scene della Gerusalemme liberata* in the hall of *Sant'Eligio* Institute in Naples and the *Natività di Maria* in the church of *San Nicola dei Latini* in Polla near Salerno (signed and dated 1805).

[4] Edoardo Nappi kindly advised me to consult an interesting pamphlet with neither date nor author: *Brevi accenni sull'edificio del Monte di Pietà. Origini, vicende, ricostruzioni, opere d'arte*, Edizioni Raimondi. The pamphlet recounts the fire of 3rd June 1903 and gives further information about the consequent restoration works. Moreover, in «Napoli Nobilissima», I, New Series, 1920, X, p. 152, there is an anonymous paragraph about the works executed that year (1920) in the *Pietà* building.

[5] *Brevi accenni sull'Edificio...* cit., p. 4.

[6] *Brevi accenni sull' Edificio...* cit., p. 19.

[7] *Brevi accenni sull'Edificio...* cit., p. 22.

[8] For what concerns the restoration of the painting cnf. B. MOLAJOLI, *Opere d'arte del Banco di Napoli*, Napoli, 1953, p. 40. Information about the restoration of the painting in 1902 is contained in the pamphlet: *Brevi accenni sull'Edificio...* cit., pp. 21-22.

[9] M. MORELLI, L. CONFORTI, *La cappella del Monte di Pietà*, Napoli, 1899, pp. 2-3.

[10] For further information about the vault of the ex-refectory of the church of Monteoliveto in Naples cnf. P. LEONE DE CASTRIS, *Napoli 1544: Vasari e Monteoliveto*, in «Bollettino d'Arte», 1981, pp. 59-88.

[11] In the above-mentioned vault of the church of *Monteoliveto*, Vasari represented the figure «Pazienza» in profile with a yoke on her shoulders. In Vasari's house in Arezzo, in the room named «Camino» the painter represents the figure of «Concordia» in the same way. For what concerns a comparison between the two «allegorie» cnf. P. LEONE DE CASTRIS, op. cit., p. 71, figg. 22-23.

[12] The last room from a topographical point of view, frescoed in the 18th century, is very well preserved so that it has not been necessary to intervene.

[13] B. MOLAJOLI, op. cit., p. 43, data about the reconstruction made by Paolo Vetri, is in *Brevi accenni...*, cit., p. 22.

[14] *Brevi accenni sull'Edificio...*, cit., p. 22.

[15] *Brevi accenni sull'Edificio...*, cit., p. 22.

[16] *Brevi accenni sull'Edificio...*, cit., p. 22.

[17] N. SPINOSA, in *Civiltà del Settecento a Napoli*, Catalogue of the art-exhibition, Firenze, 1979, I, p. 208. On the occasion of this exhibition the painting was restored.

[18] This hypothesis was made by B. MOLAJOLI, op. cit., p. 20, and has been verbally confirmed by Nicola Spinosa.

[19] M. MORELLI, L. CONFORTI, op. cit., p. 39, note 1.

Improvement and Static Reinforcement of the Building
Restoration of the Chapel

by Mario Scognamiglio and Giancarlo Marobbio

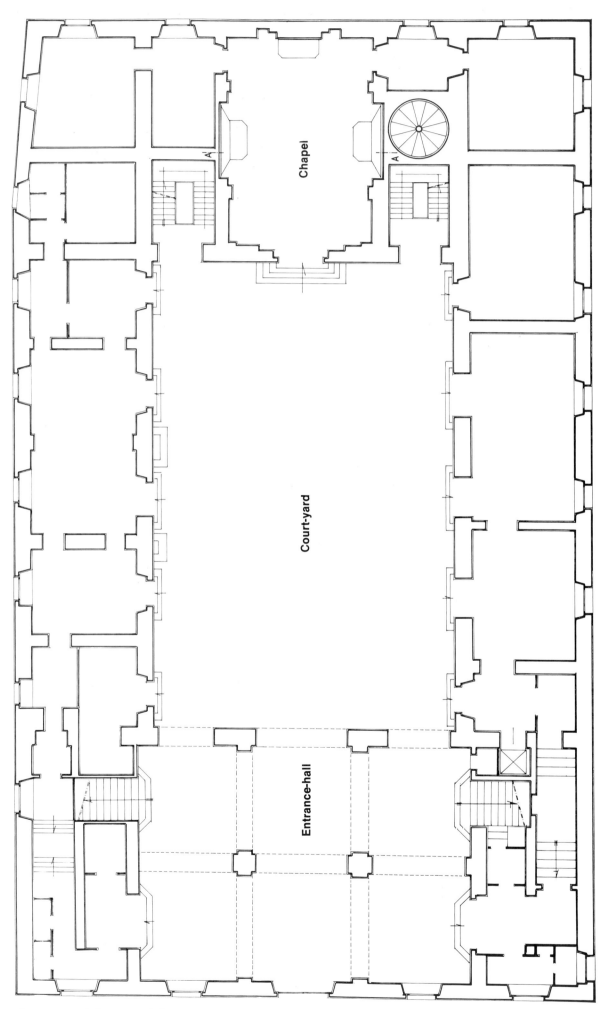

Planimetry of the ground floor

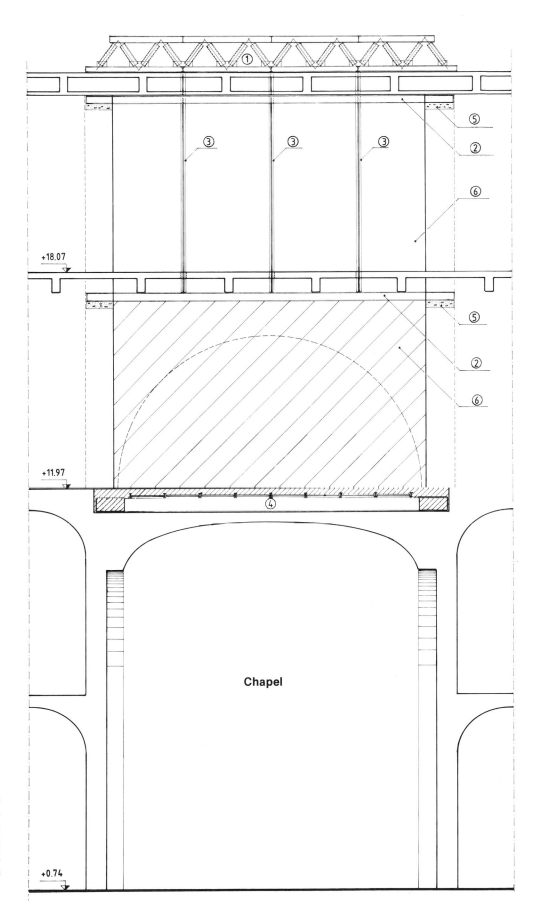

① Metal trellis constructed on the covering attic
② Girders supporting the covering and intermediate attics (m. 18,07 heigh) ③ Stay-rods for the
suspension of the girders supporting the attics
④ Attic close to the covering vault of the Chapel
⑤ Reinforced concrete base on which the girders
rest ⑥ Demolished walls

Cross section on the Chapel

The overall form of *Monte di Pietà* is rectangular, outlined by perimetric buildings and a central courtyard. The plan indicates a total area of 1,900 m³. The building rises three storeys above the ground to a height of some 24 metres.

The rear body of the construction houses the old chapel, the central part of which covers the entire first floor; the rooms on the second and third floors are used for storage.

The building has recently been the object of a complex operation of restoration commencing with the indispensable task of improvement and static reinforcement and concluding with the organization of the considerable artistic patrimony conserved in the chapel of the building.

This volume places particular emphasis on the work of improvement regarding the wall structures of the entire edifice since they have played an important role in the construction of the chapel, especially the perimetric walls afflicted by humidity. Chinks and crevices had developed over the years and were strikingly accentuated as a consequence of the earthquake in November, 1980. The damage chiefly concernend the principal and secondary front walls and the stair structures. The junctures of orthogonal walls began to split, triggered by the attack of humidity in the main wall structures and along the verticals weakened by the presence of the various rooms.

Considerable fissuring is to be seen in the vertical aspect of the chapel. The entrance façade, adorned with the valuable decorations in stone of the tympana and various works in marble, presents a diffuse series of visible lesions, especially on the architrave of the entrance portal, on the large central window and on the higher curvilinear tympanum. The presence of fissuring continues in correspondence with the central zone of the trabeation and on the front part of the upper tympanum. The architrave of the portal shows an accentuated deformation, the stone block shattered into various fragments. Further troublesome fissuring was found on the intrados of the vault faced with tufa — supporting the floor of the chapel — and in the covering vault. An irregualr static situation was further discovered in the covering vault which determined a «crushing» effect and caused the plaster, rich in valuable frescoes and decorations, to become detached and fall.

The considerable weight of archives present on the two storeys above the chapel bore heavily on the garrets, resting on a wall constructed in a remote epoch, «knifed» into the covering vault of the central room.

It was ascertained that the excessive burden bearing on the overhead garrets transmitted to the vault, through the wall, not less than a 230 ton load corresponding to ca. 34 t./m² in that part of the vault concerned. Onerous weights, indeed, for a vault, even if an «arch effect» which took place in the wall (manifested by parabolic lesions) had certainly reduced the direct action on the supporting base, favouring a channeling of the flow of tension towards the lateral zones, i.e. onto the perimetral walls.

We might add, too, that the loads weighed upon the terminal ring of the vault, i.e. at the edge of a zone with an abruptly reduced thickness of only 30 cm. and consequently absolutely inadequate in respect of the enormous weight.

The absorption of such a heavy load and the subsequent «arched» adaptment of the wall did not occur without traumas; in addition to the lesions on the vertical walls there were transverse lesions on the intrados of the vault in way of the ring on the wall above.

These signs of settling were the proof and confirmation of the presence of unacceptable states of tension.

The supporting vault of the chapel floor also presented fissures on the intrados. The presence of some supporting wall structures, located near the keystone and clearly added in an epoch successive to construction of the building, lead us to presume that unsettling had occurred in earlier times as well. However, the reinforcing structure, composed of two walls — one of which arched and pilastered — appeared neither well-conceived nor well-executed and, consequently, scarcely trustworthy and efficient.

On completion of the generalized investigation carried out on the entire edifice, it was more than clear that a plan of intervention was essential, aimed at attaining the static improvement and reinforcement of the structure of the entire building and, in particular, the vertical aspect of the chapel.

Steps were therefore taken to consolidate the vertical masonry by injections of pressurized cement mortar; to consolidate the ramps and the stair galleries; to mend the vertical lesions and restore the masonry in correspondence with the internal and external spaces by injections integrated with the riveting of steel rods (reinforced injection); to unite the orthogonal masonry walls by means of stitching with long prestretched strands of music wire strengthened at the ends with special anchoring plates and positioned in bored holes injected with additative mortar.

These seams, distributed within the masonry masses and regulated in a way to guarantee a tight connection even in the case of horizontal stress, have allowed for the elimination of that degree of detachment between the orthogonal walls, caused by lesions, which seriously prejudiced the efficiency of the masonry frame.

The operations of static reinforcement and improvement of the chapel construction proved to be very complex owing to the necessity of guaranteeing the traditional exigencies of the spacious rooms situated on the two upper floors and thus allow for their complete serviceability — safeguarding meanwhile, their conservation without damaging the artistic patrimony contained therein.

Restoration of the masonry vault on the first level (floor of the chapel) was carried out by means of «sheathing» or plating the entire intrados and its lateral uprights, i.e. the creating of a rigid «crust» able to confer adequate resistance to the vault in collaboration with the existing masonry frame. The plating structure — ca. 10 cm thick — was formed using electrowelded metallic net fixed onto a grating of steel «nails» sealed into housing holes with repeated jets of high resistance rheoplastic cement mortar with elevated adhesive strenght. The resulting thin reinforced concrete vault was completed at the base by a cuff fixed to a base slab which contributed to the reinforcement of the foundation.

It was further necessary to obviate the anomalous static situation found above the covering vault of the chapel and, at the same time, conserve and increase the load capacity of the attic floor resting on the vault in relation to the working needs of the Offices of the Naples Pawnbroker Branch. It was seen that there were no marked symptoms of inefficiency in the foundation with respect to the perimetral supporting structures and that they were able to carry the expected loads. Only the area above the chapel and the main inside wall — resting on the vault — did not offer sufficient guarantee of stability. It was consequently necessary to:

1) relieve the main inside wall by the realization of a steel structure capable of shifting the loads to the perimetral masonry;

2) attain a more significant alleviation (diminution) of the covering vault of the church by completely eliminating the wall itself;

3) reinforce the attic close by the vault.

For that purpose a metal trellis was constructed on the covering attic of the building, in way of the church. A series of stay rods extended from the trellis designed to support, from above, the covering attic as well as intermediate one. This structure allowed for the elimination of the main inside wall which was weighing on the vault.

It should be noted here that the operative exigencies of the offices located in the building did not permit emptying the rooms during the course of the work in progress, consequently the attics were suspended complete with the enormous weights already existing on them (making far more complex the assembling of the trellis work, stay rods and steel supporting structures housed in the masonry and in the area below the attic).

Particular care was needed in preparing the surfaces on which to place the structures; in carrying out levelling and layout; in opening the rooms and cutting the wall or conglomerate masonry concernend with the steel structural elements; in clamping and casting the headpieces of the beams or the closing tympana of the trellises in the designated anchorage blocks. Once the steel structure was assembled, steps were taken to «load» it, i.e. create a tension in the structural elements of the trellis, corresponding to the test load, before attaching the scaffolding. In fact, the risk of deformation of the steel structures would not have permitted a direct application of the suspended loads as it would have determined an unacceptable movement in the mansonry with resulting signs of unsettling.

As a preventive measure it therefore became necessary to force the structure by gradual, measured distortioning movements — obtained by screwing special couplings connected to temporary suspension rods. The stress applied by means of the coupling corresponded to the stress of the actual load.

The temporary suspensions were removed as soon as the definitive suspensions rods were put into place. The masonry corners destined to bear the weight of the trellis were previously consolidated along the entire vertical by injections of cement. The attics near the covering vault of the chapel were reinforced with steel lattice work capable of carrying the entire estimated load on the three perimetral walls, avoiding the main inside wall which was the last to be demolished — by further marked lightening of the attic below.

Steps were then taken to restore the main facade of the chapel. Fissuring, which presumably had been present since remost times, was remedied by frequent, localized interventions, e.g. metal claming of the fronton, or pediment, and stucco sealing of the detached stone elements. Static unsettling was not, however, resolved by taking these measures. Provisions were then made to consolidate the masonry uprights of either side of the portal by means of cement mortar injections from the internal part, and of the portal itself, placing a steel flitch in the masonry without altering the already existing molding around the entrance.

The intervention was completed by a series of cement mortar injections reinforced with high adherence metallic rods placed vertically and on an inclination in order to achieve a suitable consolidation of masonry and flitch. Using these same methods, i.e. strips of crossed reinforcements, the curvilinear tympanum above the entrance portal was consolidated. Stonework elements in the portal and in the curvilinear tympanum were restored by sealing the lesions with resins pressure-injected through tiny holes.

The cement injections were performed with a particular technique accompanied by a series of expedients disposed to avoid any possible damage to the fresco-decorated plaster through possible detachment due to drilling vibrations or mortar drippage on the walls. In fact, perforation was done with a single rotary drill, proceeding slowly and using no water. The powdery material in each hole was removed by compressed air-blowing. Mortar was injected into the perforations in two stages; a first stage at very low pressure in order to impregnate the masonry with a slightly more liquid grout and a second stage using more consistent mortar. The material used were carefully selected, e.g. high resistance cements containing special anti-sulphatic products able to eliminate the formation of saline bloom on the walls.

Fluidifying additives were further used, with an eye to reducing the water content of the mixture and making the mortar more readily injectable into the masonry without the necessity of washing down the walls with excessive quantities of water. The reinforcements introduced into the perforations were composed of stainless steel rods in an effort to eliminate all those inconveniences connected with the corrosion of metals inside masonry.

Final steps in the chapel consisted in the restoration of the perimetral mansonry afflicted by rising humidity. The lower bands of the perimetral walls showed evident signs of infiltration of water which, over the years, had caused appreciable damage to the frescoed and decorated wall surfaces.

In certain areas, the hygroscopic fringe — proof of remote as well as recent phenomena of capillary moisture — reached more than three meters in height. In fact, there were clear traces of soluble salts which, transported by the water rising from the foundation by capillarity, had remained in loco despite the substantial regression of the capillary action.

Laboratory instrumental tests made on samples drawn both on the surface and in depth in the masonry permitted secure individualization of the structures invaded by capillarity as opposed to those structures afflicted by old phenomena no longer in course. It was thus ascertained that the main inside wall could be considered generally dry, thanks to the beneficial effect of the underlying cellars; contrarily, the perimetral walls disclosed a height of humidity undeniably bound to the quota of ground outside the construction. In fact, when the quota was sufficiently lower than the internal one, the phenomen remained within a limited entity, creating no further inconveniences.

The operation of restoration and defense against humidity was mainly carried out by creating improved ventilation of the cellars, tending to favour maximum evaporation of the water absorbed by the foundations in order to reduce any quantity of humidity arriving below the frescoed and decrsoated surfaces, and, fundamentally, by horizontal waterproofing of the masonry in those places where capillary action was so copious that even the best ventilation could not reduce it sufficiently.

The possibility was soon discarded of creating a horizontal barrier to the rising humidity with the continuous-cut technique, using band saws and inserting lead or resin sheeting aimed at limiting — as much as possible — further damage to the plaster and to the frescoes. The final decision was made to create a continuous chemical barrier obtained with the technique of core boring. At ca. 20 cm from floor level, a continuous series of holes were made, perpendicular to the masonry, their depth measuring ca. 2/3 of the entire thickness (30 mm holes with 150 mm distances between centers). By means of special transfusors, a mixture of siliconic resins was let into the masonry thickness in fractional doses until the stonework was thoroughly soaked. In a short time a waterproof barrier was created through successive processes of polymerisation and crystalization.

The mixtures were composed of carefully selected materials such as anhydrous silanes in aliphatic and aromatic hydrocarbon carriers whose reticulation — in the process of crystalization — does not give rise to salts which would later have been evidenced on the surfaces of the treated walls, with obvious damage to the frescoes.

On completion of the complex operation of static reinforcement, strengthening of the masonry structures and waterproofing of the perimetral walls, the work of restoration of the frescoes was commenced.

Stay-rods supporting the attics

Metal trellis constructed on the covering attic of Building

Documents of the «*Archivio Storico*»
of the «*Banco di Napoli*»
edited by Eduardo Nappi

1. 5 dicembre 1597. Ducati 16.300 per acquisto palazzo grande nella strada maestra di Seggio di Nido da Delitia Gesualda, madre, balia e tutrice di Francesco Carrafa, figlio del quondam Geronimo Carrafa (Libro di Casa, matr. 184, f. 267).

2. 24 dicembre 1597. Ducati 200 a Giovan Giacomo Conforto e Giovan Cola di Franco in conto della fabbrica fatta e da farsi per essi nella nova casa del Monte (Giornale del patrimonio, matr. 167, f. 54).

3. 11 febbraio 1598. Ducati 85 a Giovan Battista Cavagna incegniero a compimento di ducati 100 et sono per saldo di tutte fatiche et servitii fatti nel far che li disegni della casa nova del Monte et altre cose per detta fabbrica, stabilendo che dal primo di febraro avante li è stabilita provisione di ducati 12 il mese durante detta fabbrica come incegniero (Giornale del patrimonio, matr. 167, f. 64).

4. 7 luglio 1598. Ducati 100 a Ciccardo Bernucci e Cristofaro Monterosso, marmorari in conto de li marmi di Carrara, di Massa e di Caserta che insolidum promettono far venire a proprie spese a la fabrica del Monte e lavorarli (Libro di Casa, matr. 184, f. 340).

5. 19 novembre 1598. Ducati 100 a Ciccardo Bernucci e Cristofaro Monterosso in conto della cancellata fanno per la cappella del Monte e promettono farla de fino ottone lavorato, tutta d'un pezzo a lima rifilata e suggellata dentro e fuori, conforme al disegno dell'ingegnere Cavagni ad ogni loro spesa e particolarmente nel far il modello. (Giornale del patrimonio, matr. 167, f. 111).

6. 24 aprile 1599. Ducati 6 a Francesco de Simone a compimento di ducati 76 per saldo conto de legnami e fattura del modello de la nova casa per lui et altri fatto a sue spese, così tassato da comoni esperti (Libro di Casa, matr. 184, f. 368).

7. 10 febbraio 1601. Ducati 202 a Pietro Bernino a compimento di ducati 700 per la fattura de le due statue di marmi gentili, una intitulata la Carità che sta con tre puttini in se e l'altra la Sicurtà poste ne la nova casa del Monte apprezzato tal prezzo da comoni esperti, de volontà comone (Libro di Casa, matr. 184, f. 490).

8. 12 febbraio 1601. Ducati 354 a Michelangelo Naccherino a compimento di ducati 754, che l'altri ducati 400 li sono stati pagati li anni addietro a buonconto di ducati 804 per la manifattura de la Madonna de la Pietà con suo Santissimo Figlio in braccio, de marmi sculpiti, posti nella nova casa del Monte di volontà comone apprezzata d'esperti, atteso li restanti se li pagherà quando havrà compita la detta opra, che li altri ducati 4 sono per la portatura (Libro di Casa, matr. 184, f. 490).

9. 20 febbraio 1601. Ducati 12 a Loise Rodrigo per la pittura di chiaro scuro a fresco della Fede e della Speranza con quattro puttini fatte al frontespizio del muro della cappella del Nostro Monte (Giornale del patrimonio, matr. 167, f. 111).

10. 26 febbraio 1601. Ducati 6 a Giovan Battista Caracciolo per la pittura di chiaro oscuro fatta a fresco de li sei puttini al frontespizio del muro de la cappella del novo Monte (Libro di Casa, matr. 184, f. 492).

11. 2 marzo 1601. Ducati 6 ad Alessandro Ernandes pittor per haver pintato e fatto li mischi ne la facciata dentro il cortiglio sopra la nova cappella del Monte (Libro di Casa, matr. 184, f. 492).

12. 19 ottobre 1601. Ducati 80 a Bellisario Corenzi a compimento di ducati 200 per la pintura che ha fatto ne la camera de la Congregazione e del Banco del Monte (Libro di Casa, matr. 184, f. 555).

13. 22 dicembre 1601. Ducati 9,60 a Cola Francesco Parmese, sono per la fattura di 34 rose grandi di legno e pittura di quelle a grana 15 ciascuna et per 300 rosette piccole per li falsi a grana uno e mezzo lo legno, pittura et fattura per la tempiatura de la guardarobba (Giornale del patrimonio, matr. 167, f. 281).

14. 31 luglio 1602. Ducati 4 a Giovan Battista Cavagna, Colantonio Angelosa, Pignalosa Cafaro et Costantino Avallone a ciascheduno d'essi ducati 1 per haverno reconosciuto il stipo dell'oro incominciato nella sala e da loro concluso che si facci ne la guardarobba maggiore (Giornale del patrimonio, matr. 167, f. 314v).

15. 22 marzo 1603. Ducati 60 a Fabritio Santafede in conto del quadro della Pietà posto (Libro di Casa, matr. 185, f. 296).

16. 5 aprile 1603. Ducati 30 a Geronimo Imparato in conto della pittura del quadro dell'Assunta di Nostra Signora per la cappella (Libro di Casa, matr. 185, f. 296).

17. 22 dicembre 1603. D. 20 a compimento di ducati 120 a Ippolito Borghese in conto della pittura della cona dell'Assunta della Madonna farà (Libro di Casa, matr. 186, f. 362).

18. 19 dicembre 1603. Ducati 20 a compimento di ducati 30 a Tomaso Montani a conto de li due angioli fa per ponerli fuori la cappella (Libro di Casa, matr. 186, f. 362).

19. 22 dicembre 1603. Ducati 420 a compimento di ducati 600 a Bellisario Corenzi per la pittura de la cappella e fuori di quella, sopra la porta del Monte, da la di dentro et al muro dove si impegna da la parte del cortiglio con lui liquidato per detto prezzo (Libro di Casa, matr. 186, f. 362).

20. 22 dicembre 1603. Ducati 50 a Giuseppe Mellone a compimento di ducati 80 per tutta l'opera e spesa fatta ne la Pietà de relievo per lo guardaroba dell'oro (Libro Maggiore del patrimonio, matr. 186, f. 362).

21. 4 giugno 1604. Ducati 20 a Bellisario Corenzi a conto del residuo de la pittura de la cappella (Libro Maggiore del patrimonio, matr. 186, f. 377).

22. 17 dicembre 1604. Ducati 101,80 a Fabritio Santafede per fattura della cona dell'Altare Maggiore (Libro Maggiore del patrimonio, matr. 186, f. 377).

23. 6 luglio 1607. Ducati 25 a Geronimo Imparato a compimento di ducati 55 in conto del quadro della cappella (Libro Maggiore del patrimonio, matr. 186, f. 499).

24. 27 agosto 1607. Et essendo morto Geronimo Imperato pittore che faceva la cona della Resurrettione nella nostra cappella, essi Signori Protettori hanno conchiuso che si facci da Fabritio Santafede homo di molto valore e che tiene nella pittura pochi pari, e circa il prezzo di quella si lasci all'arbitrio e regolato giuditio del Signor Paulo Sanfelice già Protettore (Libro di Conclusioni, matr. 243, f. 64).

25. 24 marzo 1608. Ducati 30 a Fabritio Santafede a conto della cona della cappella (Libro Maggiore del Patrimonio, matr. 186, f. 533).

26. 1 dicembre 1608. Ducati 10 a Giuseppe Milone a compimento di ducati 150 per la cornice per la cona della Resurrettione del Signore (Libro Maggiore del Patrimonio, matr. 186, f. 533).

27. 24 dicembre 1608. Al Santafede il quadro viene pagato 400 ducati ed il pittore promette di dare un quadro con la pittura di un Cristo flagellato per ducati 20 per tenerlo nella camera dell'Udienza, dove i Protettori fanno Congregazione (Libro di Conclusioni, matr. 243, f. 64).

28. 17 febbraio 1614. Ducati 45 a Tomaso Montani a compimento di ducati 120 per li due angeli fatti e posti a sue spese alli lati della Pietà alla cappella (Libro maggiore di Terze, matr. 76, f. 653).

29. 17 febbraio 1614. Ducati 50 ad Angelo Landi per lo lavaturo di marmo con misco e fattura, posto nella sacrestia della cappella (Libro Maggiore di Terze, matr. 76, f. 653).

30. 13 ottobre 1618. Ducati 350 a Cosmo Fansago per l'epitaffio nella cappella del Monte del Cardinale Acquaviva (Libro Maggiore di Terze, matr. 78, f. 697).

31. 15 novembre 1618. Ducati 12 a Bellisario Correnzi per la pittura fatta e farà delli due padiglioni et una penta d'epitaffio dentro la cappella del Monte (Libro Maggiore di Terze, matr. 78, f. 697).

32. 17 ottobre 1619. Ducati 12 a Giovan Vincenzo Forli per prezzo d'un quadro di Nostro Signore quando suda sangue per servizio della camera del razionale, inclusa in esso la figura che haverrà d'accomodare a frisco sta medesimamente penta dentro detta camera (Libro Maggiore di Terze, matr. 81, f. 727).

33. 29 novembre 1619. Ducati 3 a Giuseppe Millone per l'indoratura della cornice del quadro posto dentro la camera del razionale (Libro Maggiore di Terze, matr. 81, f. 727).

34. 25 maggio 1637. Ducati 10 a Cosmo Fanzago per prezzo di uno zoccolo di marmo di color bianco e mischio ha fatto far per servizio di detta cappella (Libro Maggiore di Terze, matr. 96, f. 358).

35. 22 agosto 1639. Ducati 10 ad Antonino de Simone per caparra et in conto del prezzo di cornicopie di legno indorati fa per servizio della cappella et anco in conto di quattro giarre (Libro Maggiore di Terze, matr. 96, f. 536).

36. 6 marzo 1640. Ducati 20 a Bartolomeo Buonocore in conto di caparra di quattro cornicopi di legno lavorato che haverà da indorare per ponerli nella cappella (Libro Maggiore di Terze, matr. 98, f. 88).

37. 22 gennaio 1642. Ducati 3 a Pietro di Marino, ingegnere, per essere venuto a vedere la fabbrica del formale di Nostro Monte (Libro Maggiore di Terze, matr. 98, f. 439).

38. 22 febbraio 1650. Ducati 1 a Bartolomeo Mori a compimento di ducati 11 per lo prezzo del marmo e lavoro fatto sopra lo scudo rotto dalle cannonate sopra la porta maggiore di Nostro Monte (Libro Maggiore di Terze, matr. 105, f. 474).

39. 22 dicembre 1661. Ducati 125 a mastro Aniello Rispolo a compimento di ducati 200 per magisterio e spese di legnami, chiodi et altro tanto per li stipi fatti nella sacrestia di Nostra Cappella quanto per accomodi di fabrica (Libro Maggiore di Terze, matr. 115, f. 435).

40. 5 ottobre 1680. Ducati 30 a Dionisio Lazzari, ingegnere, per molti incomodi et assistenza per cinque mesi da maggio 1680 a settembre sopra l'accomodationi e ripari fatti sotto e sopra il tetto della sala di nostro Monte (Libro Maggiore di Terze, matr. 125, f. 581).

41. 29 ottobre 1688. Ducati 50 a Dionisio Lazzari in conto dei suoi favori nel sopraintendere alle riparazioni eseguite nel palazzo per il terremoto (Libro Maggiore di Terze, matr. 125, f. 866. Cfr. anche E. Nappi, Il terremoto in Campania attraverso i secoli, Napoli 1981, ff. 49, 50).

42. 9 gennaio 1693. Ducati 20 all'ingegnere Lorenzo Ruggiano per regalo di molti accessi nelle riparazioni del terremoto (Libro Maggiore di Terze, matr. 127, f. 287).

43. 7 febbraio 1696. Ducati 3 a Nicola di Costanzo a compimento di ducati 5 a conto di ducati 12 per ingessare li vacui per l'indoratura alla nostra Cappella (Libro Maggiore di Terze, matr. 128, f. 577).

44. 26 settembre 1702. Ducati 6 a Nicola Montella per prezzo del ritratto del nostro re Filippo V consignato a Nostro Monte (Libro Maggiore di Terze, matr. 132, f. 866).

45. 18 novembre 1711. Ducati 12 a Lorenzo d'Achini per lo prezzo d'una cornice di pero con stragalli d'oro posta al quadro di Nostro Signore alla colonna che sta nella Congregazione (Libro Maggiore di Terze, matr. 135, f. 632).

46. 4 gennaio 1712. Ducati 3 a Filippo Vacchetta per lo ritratto della Regina (Libro Maggiore di Terze, matr. 135, f. 636).

47. 12 febbraio 1712. Ducati 3,50 a Lorenzo Nacchino pittore per havere accomodato 13 pezzi di quadri di Nostro Monte (Libro Maggiore di Terze, matr. 135, f. 636).

48. 13 febbraio 1712. Ducati 15 al pittore Angelo Parente a compimento di ducati 25 per sue fatiche per haver ritoccate le quattro statue dipinte nel cortile di Nostro Monte (Libro Maggiore di Terze, matr. 135, f. 636).

49. 28 aprile 1716. Ducati 50 a Gaetano Sacco a conto di ducati 120 prezzo convenuto per l'altare di marmo deve fare nella nostra Cappella nell'altare dell'Assunta, servata la forma (Libro Maggiore di Terze, matr. 135, f. 703).

50. 14 novembre 1716. Ducati 100 a Gaetano Sacco a compimento di ducati 220 per saldo di tutto il lavoro fatto nella Nostra Cappella di marmo commesso nel fondo del nuovo altare di marmo sotto il quadro della Madonna Santissima dell'Assunta, incluse le credenzuole (Libro Maggiore di Terze, matr. 135, f. 759).

51. 9 ottobre 1720. Ducati 49,98 a Ignazio Ricciardone, custode del guardarobba per aver comprato un quadro di Nostra Signora dei Sette Dolori dipinto da Paolo de Matteis con la cor-

nice di pero posto sopra la porta di Nostra Guardarobba (Libro Maggiore di Terze, matr. 138, f. 590).

52. 27 marzo 1728. Ducati 275 a compimento di ducati 675 ad Alessandro di Rosa, ricamatore, per due paliotti e due credenzuole sta facendo per la cappella (Libro Maggiore di Terze, matr. 138, f. 741).

53. 7 febbraio 1729. Ducati 100 a Carlo Tucci, mastro marmoraro a conto di ducati 380 prezzo convenuto per l'altare di marmo doverà fare nella nostra cappella dirimpetto a quella della Beata Vergine Assunta sotto il quadro della Resurrettione con ponere il marmo commesso nel muro con le credenzuole ed altro bisognevole, secondo il disegno fatto da Bartolomeo Granucci in carta ed in creta (Libro Maggiore di Terze, matr. 138, f. 795).

54. 2 gennaio 1730. Ducati 30 a Carlo Tucci, marmoraro a compimento di ducati 180 ed in conto così del piedistallo del cardinale Acquaviva e di lavori di più fatti al nuovo altare, come per quello sta facendo all'altro antico per renderlo simile al nuovo (Libro Maggiore di Terze, matr. 138, f. 835).

55. 8 aprile 1730. Ducati 110 a mastro Carlo Tucci, marmoraro, a compimento di ducati 290 e sono a saldo e final pagamento così del piedistallo d'Acquaviva che prima stava sotto il quadro della Resurrettione, e quello posto nella Sagrestia per il nuovo altare fatto sotto il detto quadro del quale detto Carlo n'è stato intieramente soddisfatto con la somma di ducati 380, prezzo convenuto per il lavoro del medesimo, come delli lavori di più ha fatti nel detto altare aggiunti di ordine dell'ingegnere Ranucci non disegnati nel modello, come altresì per quello ha fatto nell'altro altare sotto il quadro dell'Assunta, avendolo accomodato e reso simile al nuovo e di qual'altra opera e rifazione avesse fatto in detta cappella (Libro Maggiore di Terze, matr. 139, f. 860. Cfr. anche M. Pusculli - E. Nappi, Arte napoletana in Puglia dal XVI al XVIII secolo, f. 328).

56. 26 aprile 1730. Ducati 15 a Bartolomeo Ranucci, ingegnere, a compimento di ducati 35 per il modello di creta fatto per il nuovo altare sotto il quadro della Resurrettione, modernazione del vecchio avendolo fatto ridurre a simiglianza del nuovo, e per l'assistenza ha fatto per tutto il tempo che si sono lavorati detti altari (Libro Maggiore di Terze, matr. 139, f. 860).

57. 8 febbraio 1736. Ducati 12 ai magnifici Gio Batta e Mutio Nauclerio, Domenico Antonio Vaccaro e Antonio Alinej, ingegneri, a ducati 3 ciascuno per l'accesso fatto nel nostro Monte (Libro Maggiore di Terze, matr. 139, f. 991).

58. 7 luglio 1736. Ducati 79,93 a Giuseppe Mortale, indoratore, per sue fatiche e dei suoi lavoranti per oro zecchino ha posto per indorare tutta la Sagrestia e parte di stucco nella cappella (Libro Maggiore di Terze, matr. 139, f. 973).

59. 7 luglio 1736. Ducati 20 a Pietro del Po per aver ritoccato una figura nella Sagrestia della nostra Cappella divenuta guasta per i terremoti, e per aver dipinto due puttini (Libro Maggiore di Terze, matr. 139, f. 973).

60. 7 luglio 1736. Ducati 18 a Lorenzo Zecchetella per aver dipinto d'ornamenti la Sagrestia di nostra Cappella (Libro Maggiore di Terze, matr. 139, f. 973).

61. 21 maggio 1738. Ducati 6,50 a Nicola Cacciapuoti, pittore, a compimento di ducati 8 per li ritratti del Nostro Re e della Nostra Regina (Libro Maggiore di Terze, matr. 139, f. 1095).

62. 19 dicembre 1738. Ducati 58 a Gaetano Ammirabile a compimento di ducati 358 intero prezzo d'un paliotto ricamato di fiori di seta al naturale con rami d'oro, con fondo di seta d'argento (Libro Maggiore di Terze, matr. 138, f. 994).

63. 3 gennaio 1740. Ducati 3 a Crescenzo Vignola, pittore d'ornamenti, per tutti i lavori fatti nell'Archivio Nuovo (Libro Maggiore di terze, matr. 139, f. 1188).

64. 2 marzo 1741. Ducati 78,20 a Costantino Adamo, stuccatore, per aver fatto tutto lo stucco nella camera della nuova Sagrestia (Libro Maggiore di Terze, matr. 139, f. 545).

65. 23 febbraio 1742. Ducati 15 a Giuseppe Barberio, reggiolaro, a conto del pavimento della nuova Sagristia di reggiole petinate e spetinate poste in opera, restando da porsi altro simile pavimento nell'antisagristia (Libro Maggiore di Terze, matr. 139, f. 545).

66. 4 giugno 1742. E che si diano ducati 150 al signor Giuseppe Bonito, pittore, per l'intiero prezzo del quadro con diverse figure che il medesimo ha fatto dentro la nuova Sagrestia della chiesa di questo Sacro Monte (Libro di Conclusioni, matr. 256, f. 388).

67. 5 febbraio 1743. Ducati 60 a Carlo Adamo, marmoraro, per intero prezzo d'un lavamano di marmo per la nuova Sagristia (Libro Maggiore di Terze, matr. 139, f. 583).

68. 23 dicembre 1744. Ducati 26 a Giuseppe Bonito per due quadri piccoli per i genuflessori nella Sagrestia (Libro Maggiore di Terze, matr. 139, f. 632).

69. 12 febbraio 1745. Ducati 12 a Nicola Trabucco per aver dipinto lor tamburro avanti la camera della Sessione (Libro Maggiore di Terze, matr. 141, f. 630).

70. 26 ottobre 1748. Ducati 7 ad Antonio Picci, marmoraro, per molti accomodi di marmi fatti all'altare maggiore (Libro Maggiore di Terze, matr. 142, f. 796).

71. 28 maggio 1751. Ducati 25 a Giuseppe Barberio, riggiolaro, in conto dell'opera di riggiole sta facendo nelle stanze delli magnifici Segretario e Razionale, giusta la relazione di Giuseppe Isoldi, ingegnere (Libro Maggiore di Terze, matr. 142, f. 918).

72. 18 giugno 1751. Ducati 40 a Filippo d'Amato e Filippo di Simone, indoratori in conto dell'indoratura stanno facendo nella Razionalia, Udienza e Segreteria, giusta la relazione dell'ingegnere Giuseppe Isoldi (Libro Maggiore di Terze, matr. 142, f. 918).

73. 26 giugno 1751. Ducati 50 a Gennaro Buonocore a compimento di ducati 200 in conto delle dipinture sta facendo nella Segreteria, Razionalia e Udienza (Libro Maggiore di Terze, matr. 142, f. 918).

74. 26 giugno 1751. Ducati 31,22 a Giuseppe Barberio, reggiolaro, a compimento di ducati 76, 22 per la nota delle riggiole per li pavimenti fatti nella stanza della Razionalia e Segreteria e della stanza a parte della Sagristia, giusta relazione di Bartolomeo Vecchione, ingegnere (Libro Maggiore di Terze, matr. 142, f. 962).

75. 6 ottobre 1752. Ducati 262,10 a Paolo Agritta e Pietro Matarazzo a compimento di ducati 412,10 per saldo delli nuovi stipi di noce fatti per conservare l'argenti nella nova cappella, giusta la relazione del magnifico Bartolomeo Vecchione, ingegnere (Libro Maggiore di Terze, matr. 142, f. 925).

76. 19 maggio 1753. Ducati 45 a Francesco Ragozzino a compimento di ducati 105 per molti accomodi di marmo, pezzi nuovi e politure di marmi della facciata della nova Cappella, giusta la relazione di Bartolomeo Vecchione (Libro Maggiore di Terze, matr. 142, f. 989).

77. 26 agosto 1756. Ducati 40 a Cristofaro Barberio per aver fatto il pavimento di riggiole spetinate nel salone del nuovo Monte, giusta la relazione del magnifico Giuseppe Isoldi (Libro Maggiore di Terze, matr. 142, f. 1128).

78. 24 luglio 1759. E si faccia polisa di ducati 300 a Don Francesco de Mura in piccola ricognizione, e prezzo di due ovati di palmi quattro alti e due larghi dipinti di sua eccellente mano, e serviti per ornamento della stanza dell'Udienza di questo pio luogo; in uno dei quali si figura la Pietà che faccia le sue quattro principali opere cioè: I pegni senza interesse per l'argento ed oro che sparge colla mano destra, e che tiene in una guantiera. I maritaggi per lo giogo, e per lo cotogno. La libertà degli schiavi per lo Puttino che mostra un cappello bianco. E le grandi elemosine per lo Pellicano: col motto=Mutuat, Collocat, Pietas, Redimit, Alit. E nell'altro ovato si figura la Pietà stessa sotto sembiante della Concordia, che scherza con un bambino, il quale tiene un melo grano in mano, mentre un altro puttino le presenta un bacile d'uccelletti vivi, avendo ella al lato sinistro due cornucopie piene di frutta, e fiori tutti segni della maggior floridezza del Monte, quanto maggiore sarà la concordia col motto=Pietatis incrementum concordia, restando detto Francesco col presente pagamento intieramente sodisfatto per detta causa (Libro di Conclusioni, matr. 260, ff. 65, 66).

79. 16 agosto 1759. E si faccia polisa di ducati 300 al signor Francesco de Mura in piccola riconoscenza e prezzo di due ovati, ciascuno di palmi quattro alto e tre largo, dipinti di suo eccellente pennello, e situati in ornamento nella stanza dell'Udienza di questo pio Luogo. In uno de quali ovati si simboleggia la Pietà sotto Figura della Sicurezza pubblica vestita di armi bianche, col Genio del Banco che le mostra le chiavi d'oro, ed il Grifone custode del Te-

soro, e un'Ara fumante in segno di riporre in Dio tutta la sicurezza col motto=Tutior e Pietate Securitas Pubblica. E nell'altro ovato si esprime la Pietà stessa sotto sembiante della disciplina sopra gli Ufficiali subalterni, minacciante colla sferza una Fanciulla, che erra leggendo, e col Genio del pio luogo il quale tiene il lituo istrumento religioso, ed un fascetto di memoriali di accuse, e ne due lati del quadro un albore di limone, ed una pianta di assenzio, entrambi ingrati al palato ed utili allo stomaco per simboleggiare la dispiacenza ed il frutto della correzione o sia disciplina col motto=qua sine dilabitur Pietas, restando detto Signor Francesco col presente pagamento intieramente soddisfatto per detta causa (Libro di Conclusioni, matr. 260, ff. 77, 78; cfr. V. Rizzo, «La maturità di Francesco de Mura», in Napoli Nobilissima, vol. XIX, fasc. I-II genn.-aprile 1980, f. 42).

80. 5 febbraio 1760. E si faccia polisa di ducati 50 a Francesco de Mura per un semplice fiore di un ovato di palmi quattro alto, e due largo, dipinto di sua eccellente mano, continente il ritratto della Maestà del Re Ferdinando IV nostro Signore Dio Guardi, servito per la stanza dell'Udienza di questo Sacro Monte e Banco (Libro di Conclusioni, matr. 260, f. 137; cfr. V. Rizzo, «La maturità di Francesco de Mura», in Napoli Nobilissima, vol. XIX, fasc. I-II, genn.-aprile 1980, f. 42).

81. 30 luglio 1762. Ducati 8,63 a Giuseppe Barberio, mastro reggiolaro, per diverse reggiole spetenate o siano quadrelli fatti per il salone di detto Monte (Libro Maggiore di Terze, matr. 143, f. 1343).

82. 16 novembre 1762. Ducati 143,94 a mastro Antonio de Lucca, marmoraro a compimento di ducati 158, 94 per la costruzione dell'Altare Maggiore della Cappella lavorato di marmi di diversi colori, giusta la relazione dell'ingegnere Luca Conte (Libro Maggiore di Terze, matr. 143, f. 1308).

83. 8 novembre 1763. Ducati 30 a Crescenzo della Gamba in conto di ducati 62, prezzo convenuto pagarseli per il quadro che sta facendo in mezzo alla soffitta del salone di Nostro Monte e per altre figure se mai occorrono nell'ornato della volta (Libro Maggiore di Terze, matr. 143, f. 1384).

84. 6 luglio 1768. Ducati 38 a Nicola Menzele per due ritratti fatti dei Nostri Serenissimi Sovrani (Libro Maggiore di Terze, matr. 143, f. 1603).

85. 4 febbraio 1769. Ducati 25 a Nicola Menzele per un ritratto rinnovato fatto di sua mano della Maestà della Regina Nostra Signora per la stanza dell'Udienza di Nostro Monte (Libro Maggiore di Terze, matr. 143, f. 1626).

86. 28 aprile 1769. Ducati 7,56 a Ignazio Chiaiese per n. 90 reggiole ognuna col suo numero occorse per la numerazione e distinzione delle case del Nostro Monte a grana 8 e 1/2 l'una (Libro Maggiore di Terze, matr. 1453, f. 1646).

87. 12 dicembre 1769. Ducati 18,66 a Giuseppe Barberio, reggiolaro, per diversi mattoni a quadrello spetenati serviti per accomodare il pavimento del salone di Nostro Monte, inclusa conduttura e posa in opera (Libro Maggiore di Terze, matr. 143, f. 1662.

88. 2 gennaio 1772. Ducati 25 a Nicola Menzele in soddisfazione di un ovato di palmi quattro dal medesimo dipinto dell'effigie del Glorioso San Gennaro per ponersi nella stanza dell'Udienza (Libro Maggiore di Terze, matr. 146, f. 802).

89. 2 settembre 1772. Ducati 35 a Nicola Menzele dipintore per un quadro col ritratto della Regina Nostra Signora di palmi sette lungo e cinque largo da ponersi sopra il salone del Monte, simile a quello del Re (Libro Maggiore di Terze, matr. 146, f. 841).

90. 5 gennaio 1778. Ducati 327,47 ad Antonio di Lucca marmoraro a compimento di ducati 334,87 intiero pagamento di diversi marmi lavorati e posti nella cappella del Monte fin dall'anno 1767 così per abbelir e terminare in tutto punto l'Altare Maggiore di detta cappella, come per ornamento di altri luoghi della medesima: una pladella di marmo bianco, alcuni gradini, custodia di detto altare maggiore, due credenzuole per i due lati del medesimo, due fonti per acquasanta, per le quattro porte e le quattro orchestre di marmo di detta cappella, giusta la relazione dell'ingegnere Gaetano Volpicelli (Libro Maggiore di Terze, matr. 147, f. 1116).

91. 2 marzo 1784. Ducati 76,29 a Gaetano Avigliano, Giuseppe Izzo e Michele Vallicchio, falegnami, a compimento di ducati 226,29 ed in soddisfazione di due stiponi per il nuovo Archivio delle scritture del Nostro Monte, situati nella stanza interiore della Sagrestia (Libro Maggiore di Terze, matr. 150, f. 583).

92. 22 novembre 1785. Ducati 329,87 a Nicola Malinconico, dipintore ornamentista, per diversi lavori di tintura a colla ed a vernice fatti nel nostro Monte (Libro Maggiore di Terze, matr. 150, f. 757).

93. 8 novembre 1786. Ducati 18,89 a Nicola Malinconico, dipintore ornamentista, per tutte le dipinture fatte nelle nuove officine del Nostro Monte e per aver tinto il modello di legname delle antiche fabbriche incendiate (Libro Maggiore di Terze, matr. 152, f. 458).

94. 3 ottobre 1787. Ducati 400 a Luca Conti, ingegnere, per dieci piante dal medesimo formate per la nuova fabbrica approvata dal tavolario Gaetano Volpicelli (Libro Maggiore di Terze, matr. 152, f. 532).

95. 13 novembre 1789. Ducati 8,65 a Nicola Malinconico, pittore per tutte le pitture fatte in diverse officine del Monte (Libro Maggiore di Terze, matr. 155, f. 69).

96. 16 ottobre 1795. ducati 250 al tavolario Gaetano Volpicelli a saldo di sue ordinarie e straordinarie insieme all'ingegnere Luca Conti per direzione, misure ed apprezzi nella costruzione della nostra fabbrica del Monte per il noto incendio del 1786, a tutto il 7 gennaio 1792 (Libro Maggiore di Terze, matr. 160, f. 798).

97. 17 novembre 1795. Ducati 46,10 a Nicola Apice, mastro piperniere, per due obelischi di piperno nella facciata della nostra chiesa (Libro Maggiore di Terze, matr. 160, f. 798).

98. 19 novembre 1798. Ducati 30 a Gio d'Errico, indoratore, in conto di ducati 60 prezzo convenuto della politura e ritoccatura dell'indoratura così nella volta di nostra chiesa che delle sue mura (Libro Maggiore di Terze, matr. 160, f. 897).

99. 20 dicembre 1798. Ducati 22,95 a Nicola Manco, mastro stuccatore, per diversi accomodi di sua arte fatti nelle mura e nella volta di nostra chiesa (Libro Maggiore di Terze, matr. 160, f. 897).

100. 22 dicembre 1798. Ducati 180 ad Angelo Mozzillo, pittore, a compimento di ducati 250 per pitture ha fatto in ritoccare alcune figure sistenti nelle mura e lamia di nostra chiesa (Libro Maggiore di Terze, matr. 160, f. 897).

101. 16 novembre 1799. Ducati 42, 40 a Baldassarre Faccioli, mastro indoratore, per indorature e tinture fatte alla cappella ed alla razionalia (Libro Maggiore di Terze, matr. 160, f. 926).

102. 7 gennaio 1800. Ducati 65 a Tomase Crosta per l'importo di due quadri di palmi 3 in 4 dal medesimo dipinti de ritratti de Nostri Sovrani (Libro Maggiore di Terze, matr. 160, f. 934).

103. 7 maggio 1800. Ducati 112,66 a Gennaro de Lucca, marmoraro, fra ducati 225,32 per lavori di marmo fatti per l'Impresa sul portone (Libro Maggiore di Terze, matr. 160, f. 926).

104. 29 aprile 1801. Ducati 104 all'organaro Antonio Cimino a compimento di ducati 150 prezzo convenuto dell'organo da lui costrutto per servizio della nostra chiesa (Libro Maggiore di Terze, matr. 163, f. 777).

105. 24 dicembre 1806. Ducati 100 al fabbricatore Gennaro Cangiano in conto di ducati 420,10 che deve conseguire per la scovertura e nuova composizione di una parte del tetto di nostro Banco, giusta la misura ed apprezzo degli ingegneri Praus e Carli (Libro Maggiore di Terze, matr. 163, f. 922).

106. 6 novembre 1807. Ducati 12 al dipintore ornamentista Lorenzo Gatti in conto di ducati 60 che deve conseguire per aver posto in opera la metà della tela della gran soffitta del salone di nostro Banco fortificata di centrellature, poste varie pezze di tela nuova e ritoccata in tutta la sua estensione (Libro Maggiore di Terze, matr. 163, f. 870).

Illustrations

Contents

MONTE DI PIETÀ
HAS BEEN PRINTED IN JUNE 1987
BY LA BUONA STAMPA, ERCOLANO (NA)
ON PAPER CARTIERE BURGO, TURIN

THE VOLUME HAS BEEN EDITED
BY EDIZIONI SCIENTIFICHE ITALIANE